GOD ON BROADWAY

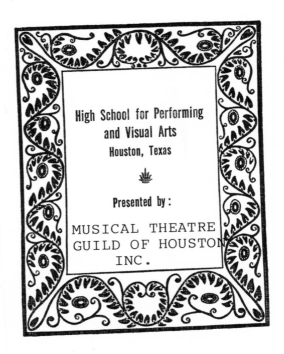

GOD ON BROADWAY

Jerome Ellison

812.509
E11

JOHN KNOX PRESS
Richmond, Virginia

LIBRARY
HIGH SCHOOL PERF ARTS

International Standard Book Number: 0-8042-1954-X
Library of Congress Catalog Card Number: 75-153181
© John Knox Press 1971
Printed in the United States of America

CONTENTS

Preface   7
1. O'NEILL, *The Great God Brown*   13
2. WILDER, *Our Town*   25
3. MACLEISH, *J.B.*   33
4. WILLIAMS, *The Milk Train Doesn't Stop Here Anymore*   41
5. MILLER, *After the Fall*   49
6. ALBEE, *Tiny Alice*   57
7. CHAYEFSKY, *Gideon*   65
8. *Hair, Two by Two, Hadrian VII, Fiddler on the Roof*   73
9. Conclusions   87
Notes   93

Preface

From the time of the first men on earth—that is, for the past one to two million years—people have earnestly discussed such questions as whether there were in the universe such beings as a Supreme God and minor gods or spirits, and whether, if such existed, their relationships with human beings were personal, immediate, and concerned, or impersonal, remote, and indifferent. Among those taking the occult side, a question has been, "How can one best transact one's business with such beings?"

These discussions have overflowed into every medium of communication including, ever since such an institution existed, the theater, and they continue into our own times. The purpose of the present essay is to inquire into the state of this perennial dialogue as reflected in the twentieth-century American commercial theater. The scope of the inquiry is limited to the work of a number of playwrights such as O'Neill, Wilder, MacLeish, Williams, Miller, Albee, and Chayevsky.

Use of the word "God," or the uncapitalized "god"—words having a variety of meanings—demands of an author that he take some kind of teleological stance. Does one refer to the primitive pagan hierarchy of contending nature-spirits, to one of its Greek or Roman adaptations, or to one of its modern guises as a personification of a natural force? Is one speaking, in Platonic-Socratic terms, of a Supreme Spirit, communicating inwardly to humans? or of the Hebrew-Mosaic Yahweh, a personalized Creator full of manlike tempers, communicating through prophecies and revelations? or of the orthodox Christian Trinity, Father, Son, and Holy Spirit, one God in three aspects? Does one take the scientific-atheistic view that gods are personal experiences projected on impersonal principles? or the mystic's view that God is an ineffable being whose presence can be experienced but not described or defined?

Since all these concepts have made their appearances on the twentieth-century American commercial stage, the author must adopt, at least for the purposes of his discourse, a world view that makes respected places for them all. If "must" is here too strong a word, certainly one can say the author is free to adopt such a world view if he can find or invent one. Fortunately, two such world views are provided ready-made—one by the history of religion, the other by the psychology of C. G. Jung. A detailed exposition of Jung's psychology is not essential to our present purpose; it is enough to note that Jung believed gods and spirits were to be taken seriously as expressions of personal (individual) and racial ("collective") unconscious forces of great power and importance in human affairs. Jung does not rule out the possibility of a Supreme Being, and himself inclines toward such belief, though acknowledging that its—or his—existence can be neither proved nor disproved. "We can, however," Jung wrote, "establish that the sense of strangeness connected with the experience of something [psychically] objective, apparently outside the individual [psyche], is indeed authentic."[1]

This "sense of strangeness" has haunted all the playwrights whose work is here discussed, and provides a common ground for their disparate attitudes toward the idea of God.

Though nothing has been published recently that holds specifically to the topic of this thesis, a number of recent comments have tangential bearing. In a 1959 anthology preface, Halverson struck the keynote of this thesis and alluded to the long historical connection between religion and theater:

Preface

"One of the significant developments in recent years has been the return of religion to the theater . . . the emergence of obviously religious themes in commercial theater . . . is perhaps inevitable.

"Historically . . . the relationship between drama and religion is a close one. Among the Greeks . . . drama was an integral part of religious celebration for the entire community . . . drama in the Christian era arose in association with the liturgy . . . *the bond is close.*"[2]

Gassner, in a prefatory piece for a play in a 1963 anthology, mentioned "Man's entire ambivalent relationship with Deity" as one of the themes treated in the contemporary commercial theater.[3] In the same year Brown gave brief mention to a modern American playwright "grappling with personal, finite gods," and observing that "The eye of God may be angry but is never closed."[4] Rutenberg, in a 1965 doctoral thesis on Albee, spoke as though a commonplace of the American commercial theater is "modern man's sense of isolation and estrangement from his society and his God."[5] A line from *A Raisin in the Sun* (1959) might almost serve as an epigraph for the discourse in hand: "In my mother's house, God still lives."

Closer in spirit to the present inquiry, though some distance away in subject matter, is J. H. Miller's discussion of the "disappearance of God" as experienced by five nineteenth-century writers—De Quincy, Browning, Emily Brontë, Arnold, and Hopkins. Miller says, in his Introduction: "[These writers] are 'a set of people living without God in the world.'

"Such a situation must not be misunderstood. It does not mean blank atheism, the 'God is dead' of Nietzsche as it is often interpreted. God still lives, but, as Hölderlin said, he lives 'above our heads, up there in a different world.' . . . God exists, but he is out of reach."[6]

J. H. Miller's essay ends with the nineteenth century and deals with British writers working in other media than the theater. The present discourse is restricted to writing for the theater and to

American writers. Otherwise the purpose of the two works is essentially the same: to try to discover some truth about the spiritual life of man in a particular epoch by considering the appearance of God in literary works of specific, widely circulated kinds.

The present author's method will be to divide the discussion of each of the authors into four sections: (1) a biographical note, (2) a review of the playwright's work, (3) an analysis of one of his plays in which the theme of man's relation to Deity makes a clear and forceful appearance, and (4) classification of the playwright's view of Deity according to the history of religion, and according to the psychology of C. G. Jung.

GOD ON BROADWAY

»1«
O'NEILL
The Great God Brown

Eugene O'Neill, acclaimed almost without a dissenting voice as the ablest playwright America has yet produced, is also the American playwright who was most concerned about man's relations with God. He was wholly conscious of this element in his work and proclaimed it most emphatically as his central theme. " 'Most modern plays,' he said, 'are concerned with the relation between man and man, but that does not interest me at all. I am interested only in the relation between man and God.' "[1] An even more forceful statement appears in a letter of O'Neill's quoted in the "Intimate Notebooks" of George Jean Nathan:

"The playwright today must dig at the roots of the sickness of today as he feels it—the death of the old God and the failure of science and materialism to give any satisfying new one for the surviving primitive religious instinct to find a meaning for life in, and to comfort its fears of death with. It seems to me that anyone trying to do big work nowadays must have this big subject behind all the little subjects of his plays or novels, or he is simply scribbling around the surface of things and has no more real status than a parlor entertainer."[2]

In the presence of so strongly-asserted an opinion, it is appropriate to turn first to the biographical material. What had happened in

O'Neill's life to produce such definite notions about his main purpose in this world? The playwright himself has provided a useful, highly condensed account of the main events of the years during which his professional life was taking form. He tells of a freshman year at Princeton, his first job as secretary of a mail-order firm in New York, his many jobs at sea and ashore in South and Central America, on the Caribbean, and on the Atlantic.

> "My final experience at sea followed soon after this—able seaman on the American Line, New York-Southampton. The next winter I played a part in my father's vaudeville version of *Monte Cristo,* touring the Far West. Then I worked as reporter on the New London, Connecticut, *Telegraph. My health broke down, my lungs being affected, and I spent six months in a sanatorium thinking it over. It was in this enforced period of reflection that the urge to write first came to me.* [italics not in original] The next fall—I was twenty-four—I began my first play—'The Web.' In 1914–1915 I was a student in Professor Baker's English 47 at Harvard. The summer of 1916 I spent at Provincetown. It was during that summer the Provincetown Players, who have made the original productions of nearly all my short plays in New York, were first organized."[3]

During this critical period, which takes O'Neill from unmotivated drifting teen-ager to promising young playwright, there is only one episode that suggests a major swing of his mind toward contemplation of the nature of Deity—the "six months in a sanatorium thinking it over . . . this enforced period of reflection."

"Man's extremity is God's opportunity" is a truism of the religious life, made so by the frequency with which people in profound trouble turn to thoughts of divinity. This alone, however, would hardly account for the radicalism of O'Neill's position, after an aimless early adolescence, or for the force of his statement of his new position: "I am interested only in the relation between man and God" (see p. 13 above). Six months of "enforced reflection" under threat of a killer disease is bound to deepen a natively sensitive and creative mind. But reflection must have something to feed on. What it finds is usually a combination of reading and a reassessment of the mental furniture with which the reflecting mind had already been provided.

Of reading there was, during O'Neill's convalescence, an abundance. " 'I read about everything I could lay hands on: the Greeks, the Elizabethans—practically all the classics—and of course all the moderns.' "[4] Clark tells us that O'Neill was "well up on recent drama":

"Even during his years of adventure and aimless wandering, he often went to the theater: as a son of James O'Neill he could get free seats at almost any box-office. He was especially impressed by Nazimova's first productions of Ibsen. He was also a voracious reader of plays, and during his stay at the Rippins' [for more than a year after the sanatorium] he read nearly all the time he was not exercising or writing."[5]

Nothing was too much trouble for the young O'Neill when he was on the track of a thought sequence. He read, as Clark put it, "for spiritual sustenance," and was familiar with Nietzsche in translation even before, two years after his illness, he went to Baker's 47 Workshop at Harvard to learn some dramaturgy. There, with a German dictionary and grammar, he read the plays of Wedekind and *Thus Spake Zarathustra* in the original German.

None of this reading, however, suggests any depth of religious devotion (Nietzsche was the world's most famous opponent of Christianity) or presages in any way the devout religious passages that were later to appear in O'Neill's plays. For this kind of experience, we must look to his intellectual and spiritual life of an earlier period, his childhood. "During his early years," Joseph Wood Krutch records, "O'Neill traveled much with his parents from town to town . . . he . . . spent six years in a Catholic boarding school and four years in the Betts Academy at Stamford, Connecticut."[6] " 'My mother,' O'Neill told Clark, 'was a fine pianist—exceptionally fine, I believe. I like good music, and always have, since my earliest childhood.' "[7] His mother, besides being musical, was convent-educated and a faithful Catholic; his actor father was also an earnest Catholic. (So striking are the parallels between the early influences on O'Neill and those at work on another twentieth-century playwright concerned about relations between man and God, that one can hardly resist a digressing comment. George Bernard Shaw also had a musical mother and a colorful, opinionated father, also attended Catholic, Protestant, and secular schools, also traveled from his native heath, also worked for a newspaper.)

These early boyhood experiences must stand as the taproot of O'Neill's lifelong preoccupation with the nature of Deity. None of the intimate influences of his later life—neither his dissipated older brother, nor his increasingly irascible father, nor his ultimately drug-addicted mother of the later years, nor any of his three wives, nor his associates in the theater—exerted a strong enough theological influence to account for the recurrent mystical vein in his plays.

The plays of Eugene O'Neill which most insistently propel onto the stage the problems of relation to Deity are *Anna Christie,* produced in 1921 when O'Neill was thirty-three, *The Great God Brown* (1926), *Lazarus Laughed* (1928), *Dynamo* (1929), and *Days Without End* (1934).

Anna Christie is O'Neill's pristine example of "the big subject behind all the little subjects"—the relation of humans to God as a deep reality behind their relations with each other. The God of *Anna Christie* is a kind of brooding female Poseidon who has usurped the functions of the fates. God, here, is the sea, whom Chris personifies as "dat ole davil," and to whose will all, in the end, submit. "The sea outside—life"[8] was O'Neill's explanation of the symbolism, but Anna invests the sea with godlike purging power, and Mat invests it with benevolence, so it comes on stage as an immanent, living, pagan god.

Lazarus Laughed, besides being O'Neill's purest and most powerful statement of the Christian doctrine that "there is no death," was among the plays of which he was most proud. When asked in 1932 to select the nine of his plays he considered best, he chose *Lazarus*

Laughed among them. There were other indications that the playwright ranked *Lazarus,* which he called " 'the symbolic story of Lazarus' brief second life on earth,' "[9] with his best work. In 1944 he wrote, " 'it manages to state a spiritual warning and hope which could be important to-day.' "[10] When he failed to obtain professional production he exhorted amateurs to try it, saying it was " 'the kind of thing their theatre should stand for, an American play of the spirit, and a play which should have a message now when death and the meaning or meaninglessness of life are so close to us.' "[11] However, since the only production was by amateurs at the Pasadena Community Playhouse, *Lazarus* does not qualify as a product of the American commercial theater and therefore, despite its status as America's most eminent playwright's most forthright stage projection of God, must be excluded from the present inquiry.

Dynamo relates the destruction of a young man who loses faith in the " 'old God of dogma, imagines that he recovers it in the sleek image of an electric dynamo and soon finds himself worshipping it with the same Calvinistic vehemence, superstition and madness. Having violated the vow of chastity made in pious devotion to the new electric god, he casts himself into the dynamo.' "[12] Kenneth Macgowan said of *Dynamo:* "The dramatist himself wrote that the play is a 'symbolical and factual biography of what is happening in a large section of the American . . . soul right now.' "[13] Nevertheless, *Dynamo* failed to capture the attention of any large section of the American theatergoing public. *Days Without End,* the tale of a distraught modern's return to Catholicism, was pronounced " 'a failure as an acting play' "[14] and lasted only fifty-seven performances of a 1934 Theater Guild production in the Henry Miller Theater. That leaves *The Great God Brown* as the play representing the most successful meeting of O'Neill's heart's desire to clarify man's relation to God and American theatergoers' notions of what they are willing to pay money to see.

The success at the box office of *The Great God Brown* has always been something of a mystery. The piece was written in Bermuda in 1925 and produced—partly at the playwright's own expense, since

Otto Kahn had refused to back it—at the Greenwich Village Theater in 1926. The whole project was felt by its backers to be extremely "iffy." Clark describes some of the talk about it just before the first performance:

> Before the play was put on he [O'Neill] asked what chance I thought it had in the theater, and I said I would give it about two weeks, long enough for the O'Neill fans to take a look at it.
> "You may be right," he answered, "but I somehow feel there's enough in it to get over to unsophisticated audiences. In one sense *Brown* is a mystery play, only instead of dealing with crooks and police it's about the mystery of personality and life. I shouldn't be surprised if it interested people who won't bother too much over every shade of meaning, but follow it as they follow any story. They needn't understand with their minds, they can just watch and feel."

And O'Neill was right, for the play ran nearly a year.[15]

In *Brown*, the playwright attempts to explore man's deepest aspirations by following the lives of two men—or, more accurately, man-symbols—Dion Anthony and William Brown, from prep school to middle age, which in Anthony's case is to death. Both men encounter and love two women (or woman-symbols)—Cybele, representing indiscriminate, universal female love and sex for the sake of their own ecstacy, and Margaret, representing love and sex for the sake of reproduction. Masks are used to indicate the differences between the true selves of the characters and the roles they must act for the sake of getting by in society.

Dion (Dionysus) Anthony (St. Anthony) represents the split, "tortured Christian soul,"[16] the creative combination within one person of the gaiety, spontaneity and life-love of the libertine and the self-denying, universal life-love of the dedicated and far-seeing ascetic. Inward tensions and attempts to relieve them through dissipation undermine Dion Anthony's health and finally destroy him. He achieves immortality, however, by bequeathing his mask to William

The Great God Brown.   Photo: Culver Pictures, Inc.

Brown, who represents hardheaded practicality and essentially uncreative worldly success. In the wild, near-hysterical final scene between the dying (dying-god) Dion and Brown, O'Neill rams home a pagan version of the death-and-rebirth theme:

> DION. *(in a steely voice)* I've been the brains! I've been the design! . . . Designing and getting drunk! Saving my woman and children! *(He laughs)* Ha! And this cathedral is my masterpiece! . . . It's one vivid blasphemy from sidewalk to the tips of its spires!—but so concealed that the fools will never know. . . . Well, blasphemy is faith, isn't it? In self-preservation the devil must believe!
>
> . . . . .
>
> Brown loves me! . . . He loves me because I have always possessed the power he needed for love, because I am love!
>
> . . . . .
>
> My last will and testament! I leave Dion Anthony to William Brown . . . Forgive me, Billy. Bury me
>
> . . . . .
>
> 'Our Father,' . . .
> BROWN. *(dully)* He's dead—at last.
>
> . . . . .
>
> BOYS. *(They file out and close the front door as* BROWN, *dressed in* DION'S *clothes and wearing his mask, appears at left.)*
> MARGARET. *(taking off her mask, gladly)* Dion!
>
> —Act One, Scene Three[17]

The play is, of course—as was unquestionably O'Neill's intent—capable of a number of interpretations as to the nature of the gods he was placing on, or just behind, his stage. S. K. Winther writes:

> Like most of the leading writers of the modern world, O'Neill is not a Christian in the conventional understanding of Christianity. Rather he is an artist who is concerned with the problem of man's relation to his universe. . . . One way he is sure he will not solve the riddle, and that is the way of traditional Christianity. . . . as popularly conceived, it is an active force for evil, a force that leads man to make dangerous denials, and finally to the inhibition of those qualities that alone make the brief span of this life gleam with occasional moments of real beauty, a beauty that would come through an admission that we are human and through a vigorous affirmation of our humanity.[18]

This view of O'Neill's striving, though a popular one, leaves out of account certain significant facets of the playwright's struggle as an artist and as a person. There is some evidence that, far from considering Christianity "an active force for evil," O'Neill's true feelings were the exact opposite; he believed Christianity contained some vital truth which, if it could somehow be separated from the corruptions always attendant on human institutions, had redemptive, ennobling power. The progress of the man and his work from *Anna Christie* to *Days Without End* was not such as to carry him farther away from orthodox Christian ideas, but closer to them.

O'Neill seemed endlessly fascinated by the close relationship—denied by Christian hierarchical authorities from the twelfth through the nineteenth centuries—between Christianity and the insights of the more perceptive pagans. Helen Muchnic, summing up O'Neill's total effort to get at the significance of any kind of Deistic belief, has this to say: "His plays are eerie with the ghosts of terrible dissatisfactions and of desperate guilt; and their darkness is hardly relieved by a hovering conviction that there is power in love and that an ultimate beneficent grandeur exists beyond the groping and raging consciousness of man. . . ."[19]

Thanks to the ample assistance provided in the playwright's written comments, and from the stage directions in the plays themselves, we have no trouble in locating the historical sources of O'-Neill's religious symbols. Dionysus, Cybele, and "dat ole davil" of the sea are all pagan gods of classical antiquity or earlier. Anthony was a Christian saint, Lazarus an important figure of the New Testament. By his treatment of them, O'Neill made it clear that he believed meanings existed in all of them that were important to twentieth-century man—though each individual would have to dig diligently beneath the surface to discover these meanings for himself—and, having discovered them, might find them at variance with popular or institutionalized versions.

C. G. Jung, the twentieth-century psychological theorist whose psychology is most hospitable to the Deist hypothesis, never tired of stressing the supreme importance of myth and symbol in human life: "No science," he wrote, "will ever replace myth."[20] O'Neill's whole body of work is an endorsement of this statement; his plays are happy hunting grounds for the kinds of myths, legends, and symbols Jung called "archetypes," "archetypal tales," and "archetypes of the collective unconscious"—patterns of immeasurable antiquity that have been recognized in all historical ages and lands and continue to possess great psychological vitality.

Oscar Cargill has done a study of Jungian forms in O'Neill's work. One of Jung's ideas, it should be noted, is that each individual has an unconscious *anima* (*animus* for females) exhibiting the traits of the sex opposite his own. He regards the rule of opposites—that each conscious trait is matched by an opposing tendency in the unconscious—as universal psychological law. With these preliminaries out of the way, we may now consider Cargill:

> Jung rather than Aeschylus, illuminates *The Great God Brown*. The mask is the face which the Conscious presents to the world —the thing Jung calls the *persona*. It is the direct opposite of a balancing expression in the Unconscious, whence the dualism of O'Neill's characters. For example, the mask of Dion Anthony is "a fixed forcing of his own face—dark, spiritual, poetic . . .—into

the expression of a mocking, reckless, . . . sensual young Pan."
When Margaret marries Dion . . . it is the *persona* she loves.
. . .

Jung [also] helps in the interpretation of *Lazarus Laughed* (1927), the supreme piece of drama of modern times . . . not only do the young men wear the dress and curled hair of the women, while the young women are attired in the robes of men and wear their hair in a boyish mode, but also there is "the stamp of effeminate corruption" on all the male masks and a "bold masculine expression" on all the female. . . . With utter contempt for the nay-sayers we may pronounce *Lazarus Laughed* as much superior to all other dramatic conceptions in its day as were *Faust, Hamlet,* and *Oedipus Rex* to the contemporary drama of their times.[21]

Returning to our theme, we may conclude with confidence that Eugene O'Neill found God neither dead nor remote. All his life's work time was spent scouting the psychic terrain whence God had been glimpsed and might be glimpsed again. Characters who claim an acquaintance with him frequently appear; the playwright does not ridicule them or discount their testimony. Indeed, God sometimes appears to O'Neill to be most uncomfortably close. His characters sometimes writhe in agony in the presence of his clear will but unable to resolve its contradictions, they beg forgiveness, confess their doubts and sins, hurl their defiance, ask for help. O'Neill may sometimes be angry at God, puzzled by his duality, disappointed in his austerity, but he never ends on a note that seriously questions the reality of some kind of universal, supra-human force or entity of the kind people customarily call God.

» 2 «

WILDER
Our Town

It would be hard to imagine more divergent temperaments than those of the trio of Catholics: Arthur Miller, Eugene O'Neill and the Yankee Patrician Thornton Wilder. Yet in their feeling about the connection between their work and God they all in varying agreement. "I am interested also in the relation between man and God," too. In nature, O'Neill wrote. Of Thornton Wilder, Malcolm Cowley wrote, "In all his work, ... I feel most of only one event [beside the Creation] that [to Wilder] means so significant change, if establishment of Christianity." Wilder himself, in explaining his writing, observed that "the central religious teachers have constantly had recourse to the parable as a means of imparting their insights to others." His own life, he told often to his "children, internal and external that he conceived himself as a special kind of religious teacher.

George has that he is a bishop's and a teacher born in 1897 and the family was had not only a teacher and three sisters (of whom one was named Charlotte Elizabeth, Wilder was steeped from birth in a general and enlightened strand of transcendental Protestantism. His brother Amos, two years his elder, later graduated from to form a distinguished Congregationalist theologian, who, after a semester at the Ecole Française de Mars II and a stint of service in France, by now

» 2 «
WILDER
Our Town

It would be hard to imagine more divergent temperaments than those of the Irish-Catholic American Eugene O'Neill and the Yankee-Protestant Thornton Wilder. Yet in their feeling about the connection between their work and God they are in surprising agreement. "I am interested only in the relation between man and God" (see p. 13 above) O'Neill wrote. Of Thornton Wilder, Malcolm Cowley wrote, "In all his work . . . I can think of only one event [besides the Creation] that [to Wilder] marks an absolute change; it is the birth of Christ . . ."[1] Wilder himself, in explaining his writing, observed that "the great religious teachers have constantly had recourse to the parable as a means of imparting their deepest intuitions."[2] His own life and work offer much evidence, internal and external, that he regarded himself as a special kind of religious teacher.

Certain it is that he is religious and a teacher. Born in 1897 into the family (He had an older brother and three sisters.) of an ardent down-East Congregationalist, Wilder was steeped from birth in a genial and enlightened brand of transcendental Protestantism. His brother Amos, two years his senior, was graduated cum laude from Yale, became a Congregational minister, then, after winning a Croix de Guerre in World War I, a professor of theology. Amos has published with distinction in liberal theology, has written some poetry, married, sired children, taught theology at Chicago, and is now a professor at Harvard Divinity School. Thornton Wilder's father, also named Amos, was a Ph.D. from Yale and a publisher of liberal newspapers, first in Madison, Wisconsin, then in New Haven, Connecticut. As a reward—or responsibility—deriving from his efforts on behalf of liberal Republicanism, Theodore Roosevelt made Dr. Wilder consul-general at Shanghai, then at Hong Kong.

As a boy Thornton was overshadowed by his brilliant father and older brother. He was a compulsive reader, wrote plays "for his sisters to act in cheesecloth robes,"[3] attended missionary school and high school in China, then prep school in California after the family had returned to the United States. He attended Oberlin College for two years (His father rejected Yale as "too worldly" for him.), then, in 1917, enlisted in the Coast Artillery—there, as Cowley quotes him, "rising by sheer military ability to the rank of corporal." After the war he finished college at Yale, wrote one-act plays and pieces for the school paper, polished up his languages and, in 1920, went to Rome to study archaeology. A year later he landed a job teaching French at Lawrenceville School near Princeton, New Jersey. He was still there in 1927, the year of publication of his first phenomenally successful work, *The Bridge of San Luis Rey*. Wilder has never married. Now between extended trips to Europe, where his reputation is even greater than in this country, he lives with one of his sisters in "the house *The Bridge* built" in New Haven, Connecticut. It is relevant to the present study to note that in his *Who's Who* biography he styles himself "Congregationalist." He has referred to himself as "a believer" and has otherwise made known a continued and deepening interest in the religious faith of his boyhood.

Almost all his early plays, Wilder has said, were religious plays, though as a "concession to a contemporary standard of good manners," he tried to keep the religious element "dilute."[4] It was almost invariably present, however, and in his novels as well as in his plays. *The Bridge of San Luis Rey,* Cowley writes, is in one of its aspects "an essay on the ways of providence . . . it . . . leaves us feeling that the author felt God's wisdom was inscrutable."[5] *The Cabala* (1926) ends with the narrator asking the shade of Vergil whether Dante was really in good standing as a confidant of God. *The Woman of Andros* (1930) deals with characters that had something of the character of Christ, and was set in a land which would one day be called holy and that even then was preparing its precious burden. *Heaven's My Destination* (1938) was a modern treatment of a classic calamity of believers: loss of faith, or "the dark night of the soul."

The intent of the earliest plays was suggested by the titles of Wilder's first published dramatic works, *The Angel That Troubled the Waters* (1928) and *The Long Christmas Dinner* (1931), both collections of one-act plays. God, in Wilder's work, is never invoked on stage or asked to lurk in the wings as he is sometimes asked to do in O'Neill's plays. On Wilder's stage God is seldom mentioned and never directly addressed; he is the transcendental God of Emerson, not the immanent, life-changing God of St. Francis. The playgoer is made aware of eternity, of infinity, and of terrestrial creation of inexpressible beauty and value. Then, as in *Our Town*—where our ultimate address is given as "The Mind of God"—a Supreme Being is acknowledged as Creator of all. The more important of these first Wilder plays are concerned with journeys, sometimes through space, sometimes through time only (*The Long Christmas Dinner* shows ninety years of a family, with characters entering at the portal of birth and leaving through death's door.), and sometimes through space-time. *The Flight Into Egypt*, in the "Angel" collection, shows Joseph and Mary with a talking donkey, who bothers to keep ahead of Herod's pursuing soldiers only when she realizes the importance of her burden. In *Pullman Car Hiawatha* the scene, as Travis Bogard puts it, is "of many voices, half heard at a distance, joining in a chorus somehow relevant to man's destiny, somehow in harmony with the singing planets and with a vast but living immensity. In the end, the train does not click along tracks to a purely local destination. . . ."[6]

Wilder's reputation, writes Corrigan, "is based on only three full-length plays, and it was made on one—*Our Town*."⁷ Of the other two, *The Merchant of Yonkers,* an unsuccessful farce, need not enter into the present discussion, but the other, *The Skin of Our Teeth,* displays all of Wilder's characteristic techniques for laying bare the important truths of human life as he understands them. He abolishes time by utilizing flimsy scenery or omitting scenery altogether. He eliminates individual character by displaying only archetypal figures —Adam, Eve, Lilith, Cain. He avoids personal crisis by dealing with racial crises—flood, freezing, the irresponsibility of Lilith, and the destructiveness of Cain. Characteristically, Wilder refers to God only briefly, but reverently, as the revered if sometimes obscure Prime Mover: at the very end, a weary but hopeful Mr. Antrobus is asking only for what God has always seemed to him willing to grant—the opportunity to build new worlds.

By far the most important of Wilder's plays is *Our Town,* the one that established his reputation as a playwright. It is appropriate, for this reason, to give this play closer study. Its first performance was given at the McCarter Theater in Princeton, New Jersey, on January 22, 1938. A few days later—on February 4, 1938—it opened, under the direction of Jed Harris, at the Henry Miller Theater in New York, with Martha Scott playing Emily.

Wilder has publicly explained that he did not offer *Our Town* either as a realistic rendering of New Hampshire life or as a guess as to what life after death may be like (This part he admits simply borrowing from Dante.). Rather it was his purpose to highlight the cosmic value of the ordinary happenings of everyday life. To project the action against unobstructed cosmic space, the play is presented on a bare stage and without even a curtain. This principle of achieving timelessness by scant and symbolic stage trappings, together with the employment of a visible-invisible stage factotum—in *Our Town* the Stage Manager—were borrowed, according to Bogard, from the oriental theater, which Wilder came to know during his boyhood in China.

Our Town tells the story of a small, rural American community,

Our Town. Photo: Culver Pictures, Inc.

Grover's Corners, New Hampshire. It centers around two families of the village, the Gibbses and the Webbs; the protagonist is Emily Webb. In the first act, Emily comes of age. In Act Two she falls in love and is married. In the third and final act she dies, takes up residence in the world of shades (the graveyard), returns briefly to earth, then commits herself finally to eternity. Emily reaches to fulfill the playwright's announced objective in a touching third-act scene where she exclaims tearfully over the beauty of earth, and asks the Stage Manager whether he thinks people really comprehend the value of each time-tick of their lives.

God does not appear in *Our Town* directly, either in person or acting through any of the village characters. He does, however, have a personal representative on stage. The Stage Manager is entirely at home in all dimensions of the mystical address, given in Act One, locating Grover's Corners in such cosmic coordinates as galaxies, planetary systems, and the divine intelligence. Only the Stage Manager has the ability to reverse time, to act with assurance in time and eternity, to grant or withhold permission to travel between these spheres, to set the conditions under which any character may appear on stage. In Wilder's cosmos, such powers could accrue only to an authorized representative of the Supreme Being.

What kind of God is this Supreme Being? Historically, he can be identified readily: he is the transcendental God of Emerson. He does not go in much for emotions, hallucinations, or seismic effects. He is matter-of-fact, practical, taciturn, benevolent, sure of himself in the manner of a flowering New England, and distant. His appeal to man, though not without some elements of generosity and compassion, is mainly intellectual. He invites man to get himself in hand, take stock, prepare for the majesties of eternity.

Assessing *Our Town* from the point of view of Jung's psychology brings to light some noteworthy parallels. "Man's task is . . . to become conscious . . . to kindle a light in the darkness of mere being."[8] Wilder's feeling of the unutterable preciousness of the experience of life on earth, his concept of death as a lapsing from this level of vivid consciousness, are close in feeling to Jung's hypothesis. The third-act limbo between time and eternity corresponds closely to Jung's collective unconscious: it intrudes occasionally on man's conscious world on one side, and on its other shore touches Primal Being.

Thornton Wilder, the serious American playwright next after Eugene O'Neill to win world recognition, comes into perspective as a kind of American Protestant counterpart of the American Catholic O'Neill. Though their techniques and their theories concerning characterization were sometimes poles apart, each was profoundly loyal to the Christian tradition of his own forebears through most of his serious work.

» 3 «
MacLEISH
J. B.

When Archibald MacLeish's play *J.B.* opened in December 1958, there were more references to Deity in the theatrical columns than at any other time in the century; critics are far more chary of mentioning the subject, apparently, than are playwrights. John Chapman wrote in the New York *Daily News* that this "contest over J.B. between God and the Devil" was "a lovely work which sings of the unconquerable nobility of man's spirit." "Mr. MacLeish has written a fresh and exalting morality play that has great stature," Brooks Atkinson reported in the New York *Times:* ". . . it seemed to me to be one of the memorable works of the century, as verse, as drama and as spiritual inquiry."

The great success of *J.B.* is all the more remarkable for the facts that MacLeish is not, strictly speaking, a man of the theater, and that his success was won in the face of considerable counterbalancing hostile criticism. Gerald Weales, wielding one of the century's characteristic critical weapons, the wisecrack, quipped that MacLeish " 'has not been able to avoid the greatest cliché of the fifties, the conviction that love cures boils.' "[1] Wisecracks often boomerang, though, and the last laugh may be on Mr. Weales rather than with him: the psychosomatic medicine of the sixties is producing evidence that in many types of cases love does indeed, and quite regularly, cure boils. John Gassner has remarked somewhat sneeringly that "we have reason to doubt that we get a better answer to the question of suffering from *J.B.* than from the Old Testament."[2] Later in the same piece, however, Mr. Gassner relents somewhat to remark that the play calls for attention not only for its intrinsic interest but in "representing some reach for moral understanding that could still be made on Broadway and receive public support."[3]

Archibald MacLeish came to big-time theater late in his career —he was sixty-six the year *J.B.* was presented as his Broadway debut. Up until then his career was divided about equally between writing poetry (as an impecunious American expatriate in Europe), making money (as a Boston lawyer and as a New York editor in the *Time-Life-Fortune* empire), and holding public office (Librarian of Congress, government information official, UNESCO delegate, Assistant Secretary of State). He has not followed up *J.B.* with further theatrical successes, but turned to the academic life as Boylston Professor of Rhetoric and Oratory at Harvard.

MacLeish was born in Glencoe, Illinois, a suburb on Chicago's fashionable "North Shore," in 1892, and went to prep school at Hotchkiss, in Lakeville, Connecticut. As an undergraduate at Yale he played football and contributed to the literary magazine. MacLeish was graduated from Yale in 1915 and from Harvard Law School in 1919. After three years of practicing law in Boston he became discontented with what seemed to him merely making money. MacLeish has written that he had always had "an amazing, unfounded conviction to be a poet."[4] At the age of thirty-one he gave his amazing, unfounded conviction its head, packed up with his wife and two (then three and finally four) small children, and went to Europe. There he wrote poetry—mainly a poetry of disillusionment—all through the nineteen-twenties. The playwright has at least one thing in common with the star-crossed protagonist of *J.B.*; he has bereavement in its sharpest form: one of his children died in early youth.

Poetry provided slim sustenance for a growing family, and

MacLeish put aside his disillusionment with America's crass commercial ways, came home, and settled down to make some money with the crassest and most commercial of all Yankee mercantile institutions, Mr. Henry Luce's plush business magazine, *Fortune*. When the war broke out MacLeish went to work for the U.S. Government and remained in one kind or another of government employment until the death of President Franklin Roosevelt on April 12, 1945. By this time MacLeish was well known, not only as a public official, but as a writer of compelling radio plays on public-affairs themes, and as a poet. His epic poem "Conquistador" won a Pulitzer Prize in 1933; he was given another Pulitzer Prize for his collected poems in 1952.

J.B. is a free interpretation, in modern costume and idiom, of the Old Testament book of Job. In considering its inspiration and conception, the following paragraph is significant:

> The Book of Job is a landmark in the long historical development of the divine drama. At the time the book was written, there were already many testimonies which had given a contradictory picture of Yahweh—the picture of a God who knew no moderation in his emotions and suffered precisely from this lack of moderation. He himself admitted that he was eaten up with rage and jealousy and that this knowledge was painful to him. Insight existed along with obtuseness, loving-kindness along with cruelty, creative power along with destructiveness.[5]

The above quote is from the Introduction to *Answer to Job*, written by the Zürich psychiatrist C. G. Jung, published in German in 1952 and in English in 1954. MacLeish's play achieved first draft status in 1956 and was produced in 1958. It is almost impossible reasonably to avoid the conclusion that MacLeish had read the Jung work as one of his important source materials and was strongly influenced by it. Many of Jung's most important ideas are implicit in *J.B.*—the duality in the basic nature of the universe; the intimate association, in all contexts, of good and evil; the uniqueness of man's capacity for reflective consciousness; the law of opposites. Jung implies that the sending of Christ was Yahweh's contrite "answer to Job," his amends for the suffering which his high-handed game with Satan had brought upon an innocent and faithful servant. MacLeish does not stretch his play to New Testament times—it ends well within the story line of the Old Testament book of Job—but within its span it faithfully follows Jung's intellectual lead, clothing it with the playwright's own strikingly original dramatic and poetic materials.

In any attempt to bring Deity on stage, the playwright must solve the problem common to all transactions between the human and the divine: how can one represent in finite human terms a power that is infinite and nonhuman? MacLeish, borrowing from O'Neill, employs masks as part of his solution. The human vehicles are two down-on-their-luck actors working between parts as hawkers in a circus tent, which is the scene of the play:

> "The feel is of a public place at late night, the audience gone, no one about . . . *Mr. Zuss, followed by Nickles, enters . . . Both wear the white caps and jackets of circus vendors. Both are old . . . they . . . play to each other as though they had an actual audience before them in the empty dark.*"—The Prologue[6]

It is given flatly to the audience that they are under some compulsion to play, here in this empty tent, God and Satan in the book of Job:

> NICKLES: . . . Shall we start?
>
> . . . . .
>
> this is God in *Job* you're playing:
> God the Maker: God Himself! . . .
> You'd need a face of fur to . . .
>   You'll find one somewhere.
> *They* never play without the masks. . . .
> MR. ZUSS: All we have to do is start.
>   Job will join us. Job will be there.
> —The Prologue[7]

J. B.
Photo from Theatre Collection.
The New York Public Library at Lincoln Center. Astor, Lenox and Tilden Foundations.

Climbing the ladder to the high platform the actors discover their masks. The Godmask is "a huge white, blank, beautiful, expressionless mask with eyes lidded . . ." (The Prologue). The Satanmask "is large as the first but dark to the other's white, and open-eyed where the other was lidded" (The Prologue).

Several things at once become apparent. The power of the divine resides in the masks; they have an irresistible volition of their own, and use the living actors inexorably to carry out the preordained action of the story of Job. God and Satan (good and evil, Zuss and Nickles, light mask and dark mask, the "opposites") are somehow inseparable. By one stage device or lighting effect after another, the playwright forces it on us as an inescapable fact that the one cannot exist without the other.

The play is made in eleven brief, fast-paced scenes. The first discovers "J.B."—MacLeish's counterpart of Job—his wife Sarah, and their "five blond sons and daughters," aged six to thirteen, at Thanksgiving dinner, debating the merits of "saying grace"—giving thanks to God. In the second scene, Satan-Nickles needles God-Zuss into letting him test Job's religious fidelity by taking away his possessions. The next three scenes depict a series of disasters which strip J.B. of his property and his family—his eldest son is killed in battle, three children die in an auto accident, the last and youngest is the victim of a rape-murder. Scene Six finds J.B. and Sarah on an ash heap. A despairing Sarah advises J.B. to "curse God and die," but J.B. is still loyal to God. In the next scene God-Zuss gives Satan-Nickles permission to do anything to J.B. short of killing him.

In Scene Eight, the starving hags sympathize with J.B., who, now sick and deserted even by Sarah, prays to die. The next scene brings J.B.'s three "comforters"—Bildad, a Marxian economist; Eliphaz, a Freudian psychiatrist; Zophar, a traditional religionist—to torment him further. The voice of God speaks sternly to the complaining J.B., boasting of the Almighty's creative achievements and pointing out J.B.'s impotence. J.B. confesses God's omnipotence and ceases complaint and protest. In Scene Ten, Satan-Nickles berates God-Zuss as an unfeeling experimenter, morally inferior to the suffering J.B. God-Zuss feels the thrust and is made uneasy. In the final scene Sarah returns, J.B.'s boils are healed, they set their house to rights, and prepare to go through it all, all over again.

In the case of *J.B.*, the locating of the work within the framework of the psychology of C. G. Jung—which the present work has in each case set as one of its tasks—is made quite simple by the facts themselves. All one needs to do is cite the appropriate passage in Jung's *Answer to Job* to demonstrate that, at least in the particular matter of Job, MacLeish's thinking parallels that of Jung.

> ... things simply could not go on as before, the "just" God could not go on committing injustices, and the "Omniscient" could not behave any longer like a clueless and thoughtless human being. Self-reflection becomes an imperative necessity, and for this Wisdom is needed. Yahweh has to remember his absolute knowledge; for, if Job gains knowledge of God, then God must also learn to know himself. It just could not be that Yahweh's dual nature should become public property and remain hidden from himself alone. Whoever knows God has an effect on him. The failure of the attempt to corrupt Job has changed Yahweh's nature.[8]

To locate MacLeish's position in the history of religion presents no difficulty. He is squarely in the mainstream of those nineteenth- and twentieth-century intellectuals who, while seeing no need to dissociate themselves from the Judeo-Christian-Democratic tradition, nevertheless are briskly impatient with any subterfuge, religious or otherwise, that fails to face up candidly to the existence of evil at the very center of things.

» 4 «
WILLIAMS
The Milk Train Doesn't Stop Here Anymore

A playwright's conception of what his work is mainly about is certain to affect his stage treatment of Deity, if he approaches that subject at all. Where Eugene O'Neill came forth with a clear-cut "I am interested only in the relation between man and God" (see p. 13 above), Tennessee Williams' statements of his central motivation are confused and often contradictory.

His own tendency to psychological morbidity is a theme he returns to repeatedly in describing the place of his work in his life. He told a New York *Times* reporter in 1965 that his need for psychiatric treatment was acute: "I'm in a terrible dilemma. I know I can't stand living in Manhattan, but . . . I need the psychiatric treatment . . . I receive here. So I can't go away. . . ."[1] "I write from my own tensions . . ." he told *Newsweek* in 1957. "For me, this is a form of therapy."[2] In this aspect of his personality, Williams is the perfect illustration of the theory of aesthetic dynamics proposed by Dr. Otto Rank, for twenty years an associate of Freud, concerning the creative effort of extremely neurotic artists. According to Rank: "The artistic reaction is . . . distinguishable from the neurotic by an *overcoming of the trauma* . . . through volitional affirmation of the obligatory . . . this affirmation of the given corresponds on the one hand to creative appropriation and on the other to a constructive victory over it."[3]

Other than therapeutic motives have, of course, been discovered in the writing of Tennessee Williams, by the critics and by the playwright himself. In 1960 he was quoted as admitting that making money was becoming more and more important to him: it "did something for the ego."[4]

Williams unquestionably noted the seemingly insatiable public appetite for "Southern Gothic"—depravity with a Southern accent—first made clearly evident with the phenomenal success, beginning in 1933, of the play based on Erskine Caldwell's novel *Tobacco Road*, which ran 3,182 performances. At this time Williams was winning local writing prizes at the University of Missouri and nurturing an ambition to write plays. He noted the mighty literary reputations being made all through the middle third of this century by writers who, as Signi Falk has put it, "believed in the shock treatment" and who portrayed human deterioration in a Southern setting.[5] As a student of literature and fledgling writer, Williams could hardly escape the observation that his own experience contained an abundance of the very kind of material that was proving so popular.

Thomas Lanier Williams—his literary name "Tennessee" was not adopted until he was twenty-five—was born in 1914 in Columbus, Mississippi, a few miles from the Alabama border. His father was a traveling salesman "in shoes"; his grandfather, of whom he was fond, was an Episcopal minister. Childhood illnesses, a sister who was slightly crippled, a family move to an ugly section of St. Louis when Williams was in his teens, discouragement at being separated by the Great Depression from his college work and harnessed to a two-year stretch in a shoe factory, frequent all-night stints of writing, all combined with other factors to produce a nervous breakdown when Williams was twenty-two. He went to Memphis, where his grandfather had retired, for a year of rest and recovery. His grandmother financed his return to college—Washington University, then the State University of Iowa—where for the next few years he studied playwriting, picked up occasional small prizes for writing, and had some of his work produced by local and college amateur groups. He received his Bachelor's Degree at Iowa in 1938. The following six years brought poverty, discouragement, illness, and failure. Williams was a waiter, a ranch hand, and a tramp. He was classified 4F by his draft board for a heart condition and underwent the first of four operations for a cataract on his left eye. He finally received a $1,000 fellowship, attended John Gassner's playwrighting seminar at the New School, and had a play produced by the Theater Guild—it failed at its Boston opening and was withdrawn. MGM rejected a movie script of his called *The Glass Menagerie*. This story, reworked as a play, appeared on the stage in Chicago in 1944 and in New York in 1945. In ran for 561 performances, won the New York Drama Critics Circle Award, and began the string of successes that established Tennessee Williams as America's leading box office playwright, a position he held for twenty years.

Whether he has retained his artistic preeminence along with his popular appeal has been a matter of warm debate, with recent critical opinion veering toward the negative. After his first successes, Williams came forward with a supplement to his "therapy" theory of writing, which he had described in his Foreword to *Sweet Bird of Youth* (1959) as "a cathartic for his psychological difficulties,"[6] and in another context characterized art as "a by-product of disease." He now discovered that his "dominating premise has been the need for understanding and tenderness and fortitude among individuals trapped by circumstances."[7]

In this aspiration, public and critics have warmheartedly supported him. *The Glass Menagerie,* the tender story of a crippled girl, her neurotically ambitious mother, a brother who in trying to help her only makes matters worse, a clumsy caller who first builds then shatters her hopes, all trapped in the squalor of urban ugliness and poverty, received not only a long run but the highest critical approval. The critics have reservations about Williams' more recent work. Tom F. Driver notes a persistent tendency to give audiences a "kind of shock material."[8] Louis Kronenberger comments on Williams' "world of loathing and disgust, of sex violence and race violence, of lurid and bestial revenges," as signs of "a growing loss of perspective."[9]

This loss of perspective goes so far in some places as to endorse complete moral upside-downess. *The Purification* (1959) strongly implies that in some cases incest is nobler than normal sex; in 1965 Williams decreed that the sensitive but insane Blanche of *A Streetcar Named Desire* was a "stronger" person than the blunt but sane Stan of the same play.[10] Finally resorting even to cannibalism in *Suddenly Last Summer* "suggests the limit to which he will go," according to Signi Falk, "to create theatrical shocks."[11] The list of items Williams has mined from the catalogue of abnormal psychology to create shocks includes incest, cannibalism, homosexuality (male and female varieties), pederasty, masochism, sadism, nymphomania, and rape. It has all been solid box office; whether it is enduring art is a question still awaiting final verdict.

Through all his vicissitudes, Tennessee Williams has never been able to separate himself entirely from the theme of the present discourse—God in the twentieth century. He cannot quite take God, it may fairly be said, nor can he quite let him alone. From his earliest writing he has made it clear that he dislikes hypocrisy and Puritanical excess in organized religion—an aversion, it should be noted, shared with equal intensity by a large number of churchgoing Americans. In *The Night of the Iguana* he introduces as protagonist a mentally unstable Episcopal priest who has been defrocked for impulsively indulging in sex with a pretty choir singer. The play contains the kind of impassioned denunciation of parochial hypocrisy that appears regularly in liberal church periodicals. The clergy is openly ridiculed, in *Cat on a Hot Tin Roof,* through the introduction of a clergyman who is timid, cowardly, ineffectual, and venal. Yet in all his poetry and some of his plays Williams brings in, with a persistence that implies its importance to him, reference to unspoken cosmic mysteries, and "the Big Question." Up until the mid-1960's he had made so little progress with this question as to provoke from Signi Falk the comment: "Tennessee Williams has had a character repeatedly ask the Big Question. It is expressed more or less in the same way: Where did I come from? Why am I here? Where am I going? Are all the cosmic fireworks just for this? Williams never gets beyond these large and safe philosophic and rather meaningless generalities. . . ."[12]

In 1964, however, possibly to refute those who had commented on his inarticulateness when confronted with ultimate issues, the playwright came up with a play, *The Milk Train Doesn't Stop Here Anymore,* that at least brushed against the theme of death and immortality. Williams announces a serious intent with an epigraph from Yeats' "Sailing to Byzantium":

> Consume my heart away; sick with desire
> And fastened to a dying animal
> It knows not what it is; and gather me
> Into the artifice of eternity.[13]

The scene is a mountaintop castle overlooking the Mediterranean. Here the castle's owner, the wealthy, ruthless, once beautiful, oft-widowed Sissy Goforth is dying of cancer. A handsome young man arrives, without invitation, after having survived a mauling by the watchdogs protecting the grounds. He has traveled a long distance on foot, carrying a heavy bag of metal-working tools (he is a builder of mobiles), has not tasted food for more than a day, and has no money. His name is Chris; the audience is led to conclude from this, and from other hints that he is a Christ symbol. Other characters are an aging, lustful, alcoholic, well-to-do widow labelled The Witch of Capri, who visits the establishment mainly, apparently, to make sexy comments on Chris' physique and catty remarks about Sissy's predicament; Rudy, a sadistic thug who serves as watchman; and a young widow, Mrs. Black, who is Mrs. Goforth's secretary. Chris, it develops, is a young mystic who, while studying under a Hindu swami in Mexico, discovered that his vocation was easing the final hours of dying people. He has unerring knowledge of when someone is going to die and feels impelled to brave any hardship, without thought of either danger or reward, to be at the side of those he mysteriously knows to be his clients, as the final hour approaches. Most of the play is taken up with Chris' efforts to establish rapport with Mrs. Goforth, who refuses to admit she's dying, and her cruel (she refuses to permit any food to be served the famished Chris) rejection of his ministrations. In the final scene of the final version of this much-revised play, Sissy, knowing that death is upon her, loudly calls at last for Chris, but it is too late; he has gone. However, he has left one of his mobiles, balanced beautifully outside Sissy's room. She reaches for it in mystical ecstacy and dies.

The critics pronounced the play a failure. Walter Kerr, writing in the New York *Herald-Tribune,* commented that "Acceptance" (the policy urged by Chris as the way to peace and to understanding) is "a not very astonishing or very original answer" to the Big Question. He concludes that "Mr. Williams has not yet heard from his Muse." Howard Taubman remarked in the New York *Times* that "the lightfingered manner cannot compensate for disappointing substance." Williams himself helped matters not at all with an interview given the New York *Times* in March 1965: "The hereafter is for the living, not for the dead. If I were coming back at all, I wish I were coming back as a frog . . . or an alley cat, or even a cockroach. If I were a little more Buddhist, perhaps I would be comforted that I would come back as one of the lower beasts, but unfortunately I haven't turned Buddhist—or anything much."[14]

Mr. Williams' play is important, not for its contribution to man's understanding of his ultimate relation to the universe—this contribution is, in fact, negligible—but simply because it is the ultimate utterance of this majestic theme of the playwright those who patronized the American commercial theater in mid-twentieth century have made a preeminent spokesman for his time. If, as the critics suggest, he is hollow and pretentious when attempting to be at his most sublime, we must consider whether there may be something hollow and pretentious about the playgoers who have raised him to such exalted estate. Whichever way Williams' ultimate stature may be

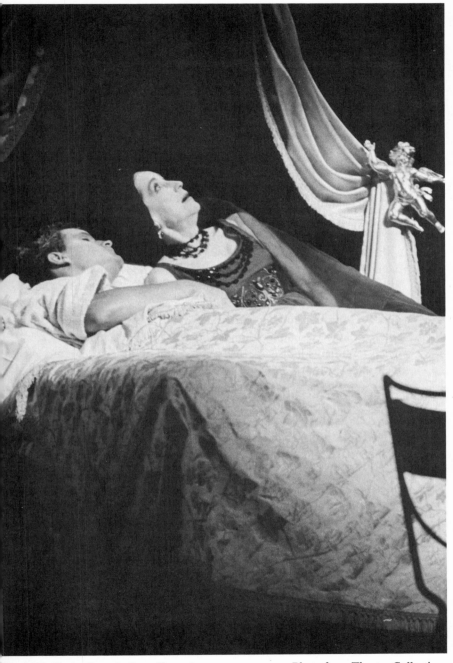

The Milk Train Doesn't Stop Here Anymore. Photo from Theatre Collection. The New York Public Library at Lincoln Center. Astor, Lenox and Tilden Foundations.

judged, his spectacular popular success must stand as an historical phenomenon of genuine sociological significance.

Historically, the God Tennessee Williams brings to the stage is the God of the commercial man in the street, well known in English literature at least from the time of Chaucer. He is rather like outer space—quite real, and undoubtedly important, but extremely remote, hard to do direct business with, and almost impossible to comprehend. He is commonly represented by out-and-out quacks, or by people who have become so saintly they have lost touch with ordinary folk. His most endearing quality is his inclination to let practical men alone so long as they let *him* alone. When some haunting intuition impels a direct acknowledgment or denial of him, it is best dealt with by means of a perfunctory salute to the unfathomable mysteries of life, or something of the sort. This attitude is not specifically twentieth-century. It has been recorded as the prevalent way of dealing with Deity in the time of Chaucer, in the time of Christ, and in the time of Moses.

Williams' work is easily classified among the strata postulated by the psychology of C. G. Jung. Jung postulates three levels of consciousness—the conscious mind, the individual unconscious, the collective unconscious. The archetypes of the collective unconscious—those intuitions having universal meaning and bordering most continuously on primal reality—can come to conscious attention only in those minds which have succeeded, at least for protracted intervals, in surmounting the turmoil and preoccupations of the *individual* unconscious. Jung would surely agree with Williams' own estimate of his work. It is individual psychotherapy—highly specific, sharply limited, rigidly personal. As such it must fail to attain the realm of the archetypes, of ultimate meanings, of man's reach for great universals. Williams, incidentally, was converted to Roman Catholicism in 1970.

» 5 «
MILLER
After the Fall

Passing from Tennessee Williams, whose work almost monopolized the mid-century American serious commercial theater, to any other playwright perhaps calls for a paragraph or two of transition. No words are better suited to the purpose than these, by the next playwright to be considered, Arthur Miller:

> It seemed to me [in 1955] that the theater was retreating into an area of psycho-sexual romanticism, and this at the very moment when great events both at home and abroad cried out for recognition and analytic inspection. In a word, I was tired of mere sympathy in the theater. The spectacle of still another misunderstood victim left me impatient. The tender emotions, I felt, were being overworked. I wanted to write in a way that would call up the faculties of knowing as well as feeling. To bathe the audience in tears, to grip people by the age-old methods of suspense, to theatricalize life . . . seemed faintly absurd to me if not disgusting.[1]
>
> I am tired of a theater of sensation, that's all. I am tired of seeing man as a mere bundle of nerves. That way lies pathology, and we have pretty well arrived.[2]

In the course of praising Miller's *Death of a Salesman* in 1949, John Mason Brown wrote, "Our need for tragedies, written from and of our times, is great today . . . never before have we so needed to be reminded of the dignity and worth of man the individual."[3] Miller has set himself quite consciously to interpret and supply this need. In his note on "Tragedy and the Common Man" he writes:

> No tragedy can . . . come about when its author fears to question absolutely everything, when he regards any institution, habit or custom as being either everlasting, immutable or inevitable. . . .
>
> The Greeks could probe the very heavenly origin of their ways and return to confirm the rightness of laws. Job could face God in anger, demanding his right and end in submission. . . . in this stretching and tearing apart of the cosmos . . . the character gains "size," the tragic stature . . . The commonest of men may take on that stature to the extent of his willingness to throw all he has into the contest.[4]

Miller sees nothing pessimistic in revealing and stressing the tragic note in life: "[There is a widespread] idea that tragedy is of necessity allied to pessimism. . . . in truth tragedy implies more optimism in its author than does comedy . . . its final result ought to be the reinforcement of the onlooker's brightest opinions of the human animal."[5]

In a discourse on God in the American theater, it is interesting to compare the New Testament "Greater love hath no man than this, that a man lay down his life for his friends" (John 15:13, K.J.V.), with Miller's definition of the requirement for evoking the tragic feeling: "a character who is ready to lay down his life, if need be, to secure one thing—his sense of personal dignity."[6] Actually, in Miller's two most durable plays to date—*Death of a Salesman* and *The Crucible*—the protagonists lay down their lives as much in consideration for the welfare of their "friends," if children may be put in that category, as out of concern for their personal dignity. John Proctor and Willy Loman intentionally end their lives feeling that their families would be better off if they died their chosen deaths than if they lived under the circumstances society had imposed.

God, in a Miller play, never appears on or near stage, either as an unseen object of prayer, or as a voice, or through a proxy, as he has in the work of O'Neill and of MacLeish. Nevertheless he is respected, and so are his agents. These latter may be prone to human error, as is the good Reverend Hale in *The Crucible,* or they may turn altogether diabolical, as do the magistrates Hathorne and Danforth in the same play, but they are never ridiculed. God's indignation is invited, not through prayers, but by showing him what has been done in his name —the method of Job, but with the complaints deleted.

The stand of Elizabeth Proctor in *The Crucible* exemplifies the central theme of Christianity. At the same time, as Dennis Welland has pointed out, it closely parallels the stand of Joan of Arc in Shaw's *Saint Joan:*

> ... in the life of a society evil is occasioned less by deliberate villainy than by the abnegation of personal responsibility. That is why Elizabeth quietly rejects as "the Devil's argument" Hale's impassioned plea:
>> Beware, Goody Proctor—cleave to no faith when faith brings blood. It is a mistaken law that leads you to sacrifice. Life, woman, life is God's most precious gift; no principle, however glorious, may justify the taking of it.
>
> Elizabeth, like St. Joan, has learned through suffering that "God's most precious gift" is not life at any price, but the life of spiritual freedom and moral integrity. [Through] her simple reply to Hale ... "I cannot dispute with you, sir; I lack learning for it" ... the learning of the scholars, the theologians, and the rulers is discredited, though not defeated, by the simple faith of a country woman.[7]

In order that the point may not be missed, it is reiterated, in words appropriate to another character's other situation, by John Proctor:

HALE: Man, you will hang! You cannot!

PROCTOR, *his eyes full of tears:* I can. And there's your first marvel, that I can. You have made your magic now, for now I do think I see some shred of goodness in John Proctor. Not enough to weave a banner with, but white enough to keep it from such dogs. *Elizabeth, in a burst of terror, rushes to him and weeps against his hand.* Give them no tear! Tears pleasure them! Show honor now, show a stony heart and sink them with it!—Act Four

Arthur Miller was born of Jewish parents in Brooklyn in 1915, attended the local public schools, worked two years in a warehouse to save money, then, in 1934, because he had heard the school gave generous writing prizes, enrolled at the University of Michigan. He won his first writing prize the next year, a $250 Avery Hopwood Award. He worked as night editor of the student paper, The Michigan *Daily,* and, since his father (a shop owner and manufacturer of ladies' coats) had suffered reverses during The Depression, received financial aid from the National Youth Administration to finish college. For nine years, until his first substantial theatrical success, he pieced out with odd jobs—truck driver, waiter, crewman on a tanker, factory hand, shipfitter's helper, writer of radio plays. In 1944 Miller won a $1250 Theater Guild prize and in 1947 his *All My Sons* was awarded the Drama Critics' Prize for the season's best play of American authorship. It was a story of a manufacturer who knowingly sold the government defective aircraft engines and thereby caused the death of many young men, including his own son. In 1949 there followed the resoundingly successful *Death of a Salesman* which established Miller solidly in the front rank of American dramatists. *The Crucible,* the tale of the Salem witch trials already mentioned, appeared during the McCarthy communist scare in 1953. *A View from the Bridge* was produced in 1955 and *The Misfits* in 1960; neither is particularly relevant to the present inquiry. Meanwhile, in 1956, because of some earlier, Depression-spawned left-wing experiences, he was interviewed by the House Un-American Activities Committee, the notorious "HUAC." Miller stated simply that he had once considered and rejected the Communists' supposed interest in creative artists. His marriage in 1940 to Mary Slattery, a college friend, produced a son and a daughter, but ended in divorce in 1956. The same year Miller married Marilyn Monroe, and—significantly, for the present discussion—had the ceremony repeated in accordance with the Jewish faith four days after the civil ceremony. He received an honorary degree in 1959 from the Hebrew University in Jerusalem.

The playwright's searching play—*After the Fall*, produced in 1964—is his most meaningful play in the present context. In a Foreword, Miller describes the play as "a way of looking at man and his human nature as the only source of the violence which has come closer and closer to destroying the race."[8] Again, as in *The Crucible*, he keeps the focus on man and does not directly invoke God. In this he is being most thoroughly Jungian; it was Jung who said, while professing himself a believer, that "the validity of . . . God can be neither disproved nor affirmed."[9] Having thus spoken Jung—and Miller—while keeping their own counsel regarding Deity, proceed with matters that *can* be "disproved or affirmed."

In doing so, Miller's manner and metaphor are thoroughly biblical and devout. Readers of Jung will recognize, in Miller's *Saturday Evening Post* Foreword to *After the Fall*, a familiar approach to biblical myth:

> The first real "story" in the Bible is the murder of Abel. Before this drama there is only a featureless Paradise. But in that Eden there was peace because man had no consciousness of himself nor any knowledge of sex or his separateness from plants or other animals. Presumably we are being told that the human being becomes "himself" in the act of becoming aware of his sinfulness. He "is" what he is ashamed of.
>
> After all, the infraction of Eve is that she opened up the knowledge of good and evil. She presented Adam with a choice.

> So that where choice begins, Paradise ends, Innocence ends, for what is Paradise but the absence of any need to choose . . . ?[10]

Thus does the playwright plant his play firmly in biblical soil. Having done so, he goes on to explain the meaning of the title and to sketch the action of the play: "And two alternatives open out of Eden. One is Cain's alternative—or, if you will, Oswald's; to express without limit one's unbridled inner compulsion, in this case to murder, and to plead unawareness as a virtue and a defense. ['Am I my brother's keeper?'] The other course is what roars through the rest of the Bible and all history—the struggle of the human race through the millennia to pacify the destructive impulses of man. . . ." Having aligned himself with "the Bible and all history," Miller is now ready to talk about his play:

> The question which finally comes into the open in this play is, how is that pacification to be attained? Quentin, the central character, arrives on the scene weighed down with a sense of his own pointlessness and the world's. . . . His desperation is too serious, too deadly to permit him to blame others for it. . . . He is faced, in short, with what Eve brought Adam—the terrifying fact of choice. And to choose, one must know oneself, but no man knows himself who cannot face the murder in him, the sly and everlasting complicity with the forces of destruction.[11]

The play takes place in the mind of Quentin, while he is trying to decide whether to ask a woman with whom, after he had been through two wrecked marriages (the second, having an obvious autobiographical parallel with the author's marriage to the actress Marilyn Monroe, ended in the wife's suicide) he has fallen in love. Miller's devices for making Quentin's inner thoughts visible to the audience include an offstage "Listener," to whom Quentin confides his experiences, and feelings, and the abrupt illumination and acting out of critical scenes recorded in his memory. By leaving it ambiguous whether Quentin's frequent use of "God" and "my God," while addressing the Listener, are intended as exclamations or as salutations, we are left free to assume (perhaps even encouraged to assume?) that the Listener is God. In this way we are shown the gradual deterioration of Quentin's first marriage; the ordeal, ostracism, and final suicide of an esteemed colleague; the death of his mother; the visit to the site of a German extermination camp—the blasted watchtower of this establishment stands in the background throughout the play as a symbol of man's murder potential, temporarily in abeyance—the meeting, courtship, married life, and suicide of his second wife; and finally the entrance into his life of new hope in the person of his third.

Judeo-Christian symbolism is employed throughout the play. Before Act One is many minutes old we have the line "despair can be a way of life; but you have to believe in it, pick it up, take it to heart, and move on again"—a paraphrase of "let him deny himself, and take up his cross, and follow me" (Matt. 16:24, K.J.V.). A few minutes later the crucifixion image is invoked:

> QUENTIN: . . . There are two light fixtures on the wall of my hotel room . . . I noticed for the first time that they're . . . a curious distance apart. And I suddenly saw that if you stood between them . . . *(He spreads out his arms.)* you could reach out and rest your . . . *(He drops his arms, aborting the image . . .)*—Act One[12]

Later in the play the New Testament brotherhood of man appears: "QUENTIN: . . . underneath, we're all profoundly friends!" The play ends on a note of Christian forgiveness:

> QUENTIN: . . . To know, and even happily, that we meet unblessed; not in some garden of wax fruit and painted trees, that lie of Eden, but after, after the Fall, after many, many deaths. Is the knowing all? . . . And the wish to kill is never killed, but with some gift of courage one may look into its face when it appears, and with a stroke of love—as to an idiot in the house—forgive it; again and again . . .—Act Two

It is implicit in the play that, although he is never mentioned except idiomatically, God is the God of the Old and New Testaments, the God of Abraham and of Jesus, and that man is the suffering servant —of Isaiah, of Job, of Matthew, of Paul.

The parallels in psychological thinking between Miller and C. G. Jung have already been mentioned except for the most fundamental one, which may be set in matching quotations.

Miller: "I had explored the subjective world in *Salesman* and I wanted now to move closer to a conscious hero. . . . A point has to arrive where man sees what has happened to him."[13]

". . . the human being becomes 'himself' in the act of becoming aware . . ."[14]

Jung: "The . . . world is now truly confronted by the principle of evil, by naked injustice, tyranny, lies, slavery, and coercion of conscience. . . . coming to consciousness . . . is a new element in the story of creation . . . man's task is . . . to become conscious."[15]

» 6 «
ALBEE
Tiny Alice

Edward Albee was born in 1928 in Washington, D.C. and was adopted at the age of two weeks into the Keith-Albee theatrical family. He went to several fashionable elementary and preparatory schools—Rye Country Day, Lawrenceville, Valley Forge Military Academy, Choate—then spent a year and a half at Trinity College.

Albee's early efforts in playwrighting were critical of a social order which, through the coldness, mistreatment, and loneliness it inflicted on so many of its members, was bound to bring upon itself a retaliating violence. His first work to attract attention was *Zoo Story,* which appeared in 1958, the year Albee was thirty. *Sandbox* and *Fam and Yam* were produced in 1960, *The American Dream* and *The Death of Bessie Smith* in 1961. Albee's Broadway debut brought him success and fame in 1962 with *Who's Afraid of Virginia Woolf?* The only play of Albee's having any immediate bearing on the theme of the present discussion is *Tiny Alice,* which opened on Broadway in December 1964.

Tiny Alice, its author says in his Introduction to the play, is "an examination of the difference between the abstraction of God and the god we make in our own image, the personification. It's about the fact that man needs to create the deity in his own image in order to be comfortable enough to worship it. It is an examination of the relationship between sexual hysteria and religious ecstasy."[1]

Normally, in a work such as we now have in hand, the synopsis of the work under examination would be given by the critic. In this case, however, a most revealing synopsis has been provided by the author of the play, and the purposes of criticism are best served by allowing the playwright to reveal himself even more fully by utilizing his own retelling of the plot. This is Mr. Albee's summary of *Tiny Alice,* given in his Introduction:

> A lay brother, a man who would have become a priest except that he could not reconcile his idea of God with the God which men create in their own image, is sent by his superior to tie up loose ends of a business matter between the church and a wealthy woman. The lay brother becomes enmeshed in an environment which, at its core and shifting surface, contains all the elements which have confused and bothered him throughout his life; the relationship between sexual hysteria and religious ecstacy; the conflict between the selflessness of service and the conspicuous splendor of martyrdom. The lay brother is brought to the point, finally, of having to accept what he insisted he wanted: union with the abstraction, rather than man-made image of it, its substitution. He is left with pure abstraction—whatever it be called: God or Alice—and in the end, according to your faith, one of two things happens. Either the abstraction personifies itself, is proved real, or the dying man, in the last necessary effort of self-delusion, creates and believes in what he knows does not exist.[2]

The story is developed on stage with the aid of a large assortment of dramaturgic machinery. The opening faintly suggests a baldly irreverent version of the book-of-Job situation, with a cardinal and a lawyer, both scoundrels, playing God and Satan, and Julian, their suffering pawn, playing Job. Alice, an attractive young woman, is surrogate for Tiny Alice, a deity with certain malevolent features. The

Tiny Alice. Photo: Alix Jeffry Studio.

action takes place in a castle in Italy. In the hall of the castle stands a replica of the castle, a kind of doll's house. The presence in the castle of Tiny Alice, the deity, is indicated by a light shining in the replica; in whatever room the light appears in the replica, there, in the actual castle, is Tiny Alice. A marriage is effected between Julian and Alice, beautiful human surrogate for Tiny Alice. But since the real marriage is with Tiny Alice herself, and since she is not human, but a deity, Julian must die in order that the marriage may be consummated. Accordingly, at the end of the play, Julian is shot and left to die, falling in the position of crucifixion. All this is brought about in order that the church may receive a large sum of money—the deity's agreed payment for cooperating with her wishes. As his death approaches, Julian complains of being cold, appeals hysterically to Alice as God, and feels lonely; the light in the replica descends from the tower to the room in which Julian awaits his death; there are sound effects of heavy breathing and heartbeats, then darkness and silence.

A majority of the influential critics agreed that the piece was theatrically effective. Opinions about the value of the play's meaning-content diverged. "Critical reactions," said *Time* magazine in a roundup of reviews, "went from 'far and away the most significant play on Broadway this year' to 'a clutter of confused thought.' "[3]

The comment of Philip Roth in the *New York Review of Books* is the most interesting from the psychoanalytical point of view: "Tiny Alice is a homosexual daydream in which the celibate male is tempted and seduced by the overpowering female, only to be betrayed by the male lover and murdered by the cruel law ... In the end the playwright likens him to Jesus Christ—and all because he has had to suffer the martyrdom of heterosexual love."[4]

Mr. Albee's reaction to this suggestion, reported by M. E. Rutenberg, then associated with the Yale University School of Drama, is significant. Just after having remarked that a favorable review of his work was "absolutely lovely," Albee protests indignantly that "Mr. Roth's hysteria has no basis in fact ... I'm sorry for him ... no validity to the hysterical charges ... I really don't know what was bugging the poor man."⁵ Since the Roth review seemed calm enough, one is inclined to ask who is hysterical, Mr. Roth or Mr. Albee?

Certainly Mr. Roth's suggestion is well-grounded in psychological theory. The classical explanation of homosexuality fixes its cause in the overwhelming effect of a dominant mother-figure on the infant male during the formative, plastic, defenseless years. In maturity the affected individual, rendered unable by early conditioning to act out a dominant male role, exhibits feminine mannerisms, while at the same time unconsciously harboring feelings of fear and hatred surrounding memories of the powerful female who robbed him of a good part of his male heritage. Mr. Roth's suggestion is valid. Not only is the fantasy of the all-powerful female whose will cannot be resisted clearly present in *Tiny Alice,* but she is also manifest in Albee's previous play *Who's Afraid of Virginia Woolf?;* the very title suggests the same psychic constellation.

Albee's notions about God may quite easily be located within the history of religious thought by means of the final sentences of the synopsis previously quoted: " . . . union with *the abstraction,* rather than *man-made image of it, its substitution.* He is left with pure abstraction—whatever it be called: God or Alice—and in the end, according to your faith, one of two things happens. Either the abstraction personifies itself, is proved real, or the dying man, in *the last necessary effort of self-delusion,* creates and believes in *what he knows does not exist.*

It is, you see, a perfectly straightforward story . . ."⁶ (italics added). Such glibness, such certainty of formula, such cavalier dismissal of man's accumulated efforts in philosophy and metaphysics, mark it as unmistakable early-Freudian, with influences of turn-of-the-century psychoanalytic atheism. Freud himself, it is interesting to note, was by no means so cocksure about these matters. In 1911 he wrote to Jung, "In matters of occultism I have become humble ever since the great lesson I received from Ferenczi's experiences. . . . I do not do so gladly. But my hubris has been shattered."⁷ Much later in his career Freud wrote in *Beyond the Pleasure Principle:* "We must be patient and await fresh methods and occasions of research. We must be ready, too, to abandon a path that we have followed for a time, if it seems to be leading to no good end. Only believers, who demand that science shall be a substitute for the catechism they have given up, will blame an investigator for developing or even transforming his views."[8]

God to Edward Albee is an "abstraction," a word defined in a standard dictionary as "a visionary notion." God is "a self-delusion" which "does not exist." This God appears to man in the form of an almost omnipotent female fantasy, mainly malevolent, but with possibly beneficent side effects due to her liberal distribution of money. She is capable of producing such physical phenomena as chills, the sound of heavy breathing, and imagined sounds of heartbeats.

In Jungian psychology, this God is identical with the archetypal Great Mother. This horrendous figure appears again and again through the history of pagan literature and religion. It is described by Jung as an "inner feminine figure [that] plays a typical, or archetypal, role in the unconscious of a man. . . .

"At first it was the negative aspect of [this] anima that most impressed me. I felt a little awed by her. It was like the feeling of an invisible presence in the room . . . full of a deep cunning."[9] These images, Jung warns, are potentially dangerous, in that they are capable of upsetting an individual's mental balance: one may be "trapped . . . in its thicket, strangled. . . ."

> We allow the images to rise up, and maybe we wonder about them, but that is all. We do not take the trouble to . . . draw ethical conclusions from them. This stopping-short conjures up the negative effects of the unconscious.
>
> Insight . . . must be converted into an ethical obligation. Not to do so is to fall prey to the power principle, and this produces dangerous effects which are destructive not only to others but even to the knower. The images of the unconscious place a great responsibility upon a man. Failure to understand them, or a

shirking of ethical responsibility, deprives him of his wholeness and imposes a painful fragmentariness on his life.[10]

It is hard to conceive a more concise account of what apparently happened to Edward Albee in the course of composing *Tiny Alice*. His comprehension and his ideology proved totally inadequate to cope with the intensity of the overwhelming female image that arose before him and mere technique proved an insufficient substitute. The image prevailed, uncontrolled, and Albee was "trapped . . . in its thicket, strangled. . . ."

» 7 «
CHAYEFSKY
Gideon

Paddy Chayefsky's play *Gideon*, produced on Broadway in November 1961, is a dramatization of the Old Testament story of the clumsy Jew out of whom God made a hero in order to demonstrate his favor and potency before all the Israelite tribes. This play here appears out of chronological sequence so that it may have the position of emphasis it deserves in twentieth-century religious drama. Like *J.B.*, *Gideon* depicts an encounter between God and man in which God is affected, possibly even altered in his fundamental nature, by the reflective consciousness and stubborn, sometimes even ethical, independence of man.

The play opens on a desert scene of 1100 B.C., with the elders of a nomadic Israelite tribe trying to sacrifice an animal to the pagan god Baal, and making a botch of the job. The good-natured young giant Gideon, known because of his ineptness as a kind of camp clown, and accepting his butterfinger role with good grace, is approached—greatly to his surprise—by an angel visible to no one else. Gideon, says the angel, speaking as the personification of Yahweh, has been chosen by the Almighty to lead the Israelites to victory over the Midianites, who at this moment are a deadly military threat. Over Gideon's protests of his own incompetence, the angel gives directions.

Gideon, complying, causes the trumpets to be blown and, on the Lord's command, assembles a large but poorly-armed Israelite army. The angel orders that most of this force be sent home. A small force, by creating a midnight din, throws the enemy into such panic and confusion that the Midianites fight, and quickly exterminate one another. The adulation heaped upon Gideon arouses his hubris. He begins to find the angel's commands irksome and restricting, and asks God that the relationship of mutual loyalty between them be ended.

Their immediate quarrel is over the execution of the elders of the defeated enemy tribes. Gideon is ordered by the angel to execute them, and finds, because of an innate compassion he cannot suppress, that he is unable to obey. In a great speech on death and eternity, the angel pleads:

> ... the bulk of men ... fear death. ... But, in truth, there isn't anything to it at all. Nothing happens, nothing changes; the essence of things goes on. ... you measure things in time, but there is no time in truth. ... The slaying of seventy-seven elders happens but it does not happen, for they live even so and have died before, and all is now, which was and is forever.—Act Two, Scene One[1]

Gideon, still unable to comply, confesses that he fears God more than he loves him and repeats his request for release from their covenant. The angel refuses, whereupon Gideon says, "I would pretend that you were not" (Act Two, Scene Two).[2] The angel reviews this logic from the divine point of view sardonically:

> Let me review this. You would pretend God is not, although you know that he is, so that you might be a significant creature which you know you are not. Oh! This is beyond even God's understanding!—Act Two, Scene Two[3]

Gideon finally resolves the situation by obstinately pretending he does not see the angel and by taking up his worldly affairs in the immemorial human way. The angel, after hurling some formidable

Gideon.   Photo by Fred Fehl.

threats, finally closes the play on a good-humored note, apparently agreeing to leave man alone for a time, to come to terms with his own foolhardiness:

> God no more believes it odd
> That man cannot believe in God,
> Man believes the best he can,
> Which means, it seems, belief in man.
> Then let him don my gold ephod
> And let him be a proper god.
> Well, let him try it anyway.
> With this conceit, we end the play.—Act Two, Scene Two[4]

The New York critics were in general friendly. Richard Watts, Jr. noted in the New York *Post* that the piece "has distinction and a haunting fascination," that it is a "searching contemplation of the relationship between God and man," and that "despite a second-act decline" it was "a powerful and provocative play." Robert Coleman commented in the *Mirror* that *Gideon* was "notably successful," "powerful and often humorous," "thoughtful, intelligent and stirring." John Chapman told *News* readers it was "inexplicably hypnotic drama . . . a lovely play." John McClain reported in the *Journal-American* that it was "a play of enormous power, humor and persuasion" with "exceptional warmth, wit and dimension," and that it was "an unqualified hit." In the *Herald-Tribune* Walter Kerr wrote grudgingly that "The form is so attractive that one can only lament its standing still." Howard Taubman, in the New York *Times,* observed that *Gideon* has "the freshness and keenness of a modern man asking questions about himself and his place in a vast universe." John Gassner, in a note explaining the play's inclusion in a collection of the best plays of the five-year period 1958–1963, wrote: "one could find a profundity of sorts and more than a little relevance to the present precarious age of runaway knowledge and mechanics. . . . But the prime experience for those who did not reject the play must surely have been a rueful sense of the attraction-repulsion relationship of God and Man in history, as well as of course in that immensely human document the Old Testament...."[5] The playwright came by his Old Testament insights through his early upbringing. Paddy Chayefsky was born into the family of an orthodox Jewish dairy manager in the Bronx in 1923. He attended public elementary schools and was graduated from DeWitt Clinton High School, and then from the City College of New York. While serving as a private in World War II he stepped on a land mine in Germany. In the hospital recovering from his injury he wrote the book and lyrics for the army musical *No T.O. for Love*. This job attracted the attention of Garson Kanin, who invited Chayefsky to assist in preparing the award-winning documentary *True Glory*. After the war, and after a brief stint in his uncle's print shop, Chayefsky began writing for movies, radio, and television. He first attracted wide public attention with the television play *Marty*, which proved as successful when made into a movie as it was as a TV script. Chayefsky's first play for Broadway, *Middle of the Night*—the story of a romance between a middle-aged widower and an unhappily married young woman—ran for almost two years, was then produced as a motion picture, and in this form was chosen as the official U.S. film entered in the Cannes Film Festival.

The God Chayefsky brings on stage in *Gideon* is, with very few alterations, Yahweh of the Old Testament. He is "a jealous God" (Exod. 20:5, K.J.V.). He demands strict loyalty: "Thou shalt have no other gods before me" (Exod. 20:3, K.J.V.). He is harsh with transgressors, taking out his vengeance "unto the third and fourth *generation*" (Exod. 20:5, K.J.V.). The changes Chayefsky has made in Yahweh, though few, are significant. Chayefsky's Yahweh is capable of a wry, kindly humor of a kind a little beyond the reach of the Old Testament, as in the previously mentioned exclamation, "This is beyond even God's understanding!"[6] Even more significantly, he is fully aware of atheistic arguments of a kind that did not exist at the time of Gideon but belong to the nineteenth century:

JOASH. . . . We are all men of reason here . . . and need not explain all things in supernatural ways. The savage will say God gave us into the hand of the Midianites . . . but was it not in fact the economic conditions of drought in the desert that drove the Midianites upon us? . . . who is this Yahweh of Gideon's? Has anyone seen him or heard his words? . . . It was Hezekiah's contention, Gideon, that Yahweh was a masterful fiction you created to inspirit the troops . . .

THE ANGEL *(roaring).* Gideon! Will you countenance this pomander of utter nonsense?

. . . . .

GIDEON. Well, Hezekiah is well spoken of as a scholar. He knows all about the ecliptic of the sun as it revolves around the earth.

THE ANGEL. The sun does not revolve around the earth, you imbecile; the earth revolves about the sun.—Act Two, Scene Two[7]

Chayefsky's play *Gideon* says in dramatic terms what C. G. Jung says in prose in his *Modern Man in Search of a Soul:* that man, by driving irrational unconscious forces out of his mind, has placed himself in a hazardous stance. Jung speaks of " . . . the modern spirit of commitment to a practical world . . ." and of a "belief in the body" that "cannot tolerate an outlook that denies the body in the name of the spirit. . . ."[8] But rationality has not served man well in the twentieth century: the more he has exalted rationality, the more he has threatened irrationally to destroy himself.

We must therefore, according to Jung, give more heed to the irrational. This, in his psychology, makes its appearance, among other ways, in the form of archetypes of the individual and collective unconscious. Here we distinguish between God, whose objective existence according to Jung "can be neither affirmed nor denied," and the archetype of God, a psychic entity found as a clinical reality. This archetype of God corresponds closely to Chayefsky's Yahweh. Jung says "... I attribute a positive value to all religions. In their symbolism I recognize those figures which I have met in the dreams and fantasies of my patients."[9]

By shutting irrational, unconscious forces out of his mind to concentrate on a practical world, man has exposed himself to the constant danger of finding his practical world overwhelmed by these very forces. Denied the chance to work with man, they work against him. In *Gideon* Yahweh, symbolizing these forces, opines, "Well, let him try it anyway" (Act Two, Scene Two).[10] Here, as in Jung's writings, the implication is strong that the experiment will not work out, and that neither God nor man will be content until a better expedient is found.

» 8 «

Hair
Two by Two
Hadrian VII
Fiddler on the Roof

Three Broadway offerings—*Hadrian VII, Fiddler on the Roof,* and *Two by Two*—plus *Hair,* which had off-Broadway beginnings—bring us into the 1970's and strongly foreshadow the theatrical relations between man and Deity for the rest of the century.

This lineup directs our attention to the fact that the three unequivocally religious musicals that have won Broadway approval—*Gideon, Fiddler on the Roof,* and *Two by Two*—were all written by New Yorkers of Jewish upbringing. *Gideon,* as we have noted, was written by the son of an orthodox Jewish dairy manager of the Bronx. *Fiddler on the Roof* is based on the stories of the Yiddish writer Sholem Aleichem (Solomon Rabinowitz) who spent his last years in New York City. *Two by Two* is based on a 1954 play *The Flowering Peach,* a modern retelling of the story of Noah and the Flood, by Clifford Odets, son of a Jewish advertising man of the Bronx.

What turmoil so raged in the hearts of these talented products of Judaism as to drive them to attempt the nearly impossible feat of conveying profound religious themes through the cynical, box office-oriented Broadway musical comedy stage? What elements of universality drew so notable a response from so many hundreds of thousands of theatergoers, of such varying backgrounds, in an age so conspicuously lacking in shared beliefs?

Clifford Odets was born in Philadelphia in 1906. "His best work, *The Flowering Peach,*" writes Edward Murray, author of the ablest commentary on the playwright's work, "projects a deep inner conflict that is also *our* conflict."[1] The origins of at least some of Odets' conflicts are not hard to trace. As a boy he was continually at war with his father; as an adult he was constantly at war with himself. Murray gives us glimpses of this strife between father and son:

> Odets found Morris High School in New York "a waste of time," and quit after two years. It was the hope of the elder Odets that his son would join his advertising business and become a copywriter. Instead Clifford wrote poetry. On one occasion Louis Odets furiously exploded and smashed his son's typewriter. "Believe me," Odets said once, "there were some very gloomy evenings." . . . After one of their discords Odets told his father: "You can't harness me to a truck—can't you see I'm not a truck horse?" Finally Louis Odets compromised and gave his son permission to become an actor.[2]

The Odets family lived in Philadelphia, where Louis had a minor job in the Curtis Publishing Company's printing plant, until Clifford was six, when they moved to New York. Here Louis drove ahead so rapidly that by the time Clifford reached high school his father owned a printing plant and an advertising agency (He sold the latter in 1936 for $200,000.). Clifford was warmly attached to his mother who died when the boy was eleven.

It is tempting, and perhaps not too wide the mark, to speculate that the playwright's love-hate relationship with capitalism, reflected in such proletarian plays as *Waiting for Lefty* and in his later reversion into commercial Hollywood money-grubbing, was an extension of his love-hate relationship with his capitalist father. In any event, after an unhappy adolescence (Odets claimed to have attempted suicide three times before he was twenty-five—"and was twice saved by total strangers"; there is no question that he spent several of the Depression years in solitary, poverty-ridden misery.) Clifford came into his own in 1935, when his *Waiting for Lefty* was played to wildly enthusiastic audiences at the Civic Repertory Theater on Fourteenth Street.

Odets' quick rise to the status of America's most influential playwright, his brief marriage to and divorce from Louise Rainer, his marriage to Betty Grayson and the birth of their two children, his long decline into Hollywood hack work, and his death from cancer in 1963, are material for more extensive biographical treatment than this context allows. Here we need only note that in 1954, after years of commercial mediocrity in California, he threw himself into themes of a scope he had never before attempted, and, to the consternation of his colleagues no less than of his critics, produced his last, greatest, most mature, and most profound play, *The Flowering Peach*.

Odets gives us a tribal, authoritarian Noah and a tribal, authoritarian God. Franz Winkler, a New York physician and one of the most competent interpreters of the psychology of C. G. Jung, has this to say about the state of human consciousness during the tribal prehistory from which the story of Noah and the Ark comes down to us:

> The history of man is the history of his consciousness. Of all the literature in the world, the Biblical stories offer perhaps the most impressive picture of a pure intuitive consciousness; for one cannot "hear" the voice of God with one's physical ear nor "see" the "Garden of Eden" with one's physical eye. . . . man lived in perfect harmony with his Creator. Still capable of hearing the inner word . . . he understood the true nature of the creatures around him, and could . . . give names to them. . . . In that state man comprehended the world within, but was blind to the world without.[3]

Possessing a primitive, intuitive consciousness which is inwardly open to the Creator, Odets' Noah has less trouble communicating with God through dreams, visions, and telepathy than with his sophisticated children in direct conversation. In portraying God and Noah, Odets faithfully follows the Bible; in drawing Noah's wife, sons, and daughters-in-law, he gives us quarrelsome and passionate human beings who, like those of the 1950's, are torn by the unsolved problems of survival.

There is a time-lapse of sixteen years. *The Flowering Peach* is long forgotten. Odets is dead. Richard Rodgers, musical collaborator in a string of hits ranging from *Oklahoma* and *South Pacific* to *Carousel* and *The Sound of Music,* casting about for something new, recalls that *The Flowering Peach* was first conceived as an opera, develops a hunch that Danny Kaye would make an interesting operatic Noah, and puts the question to the famous comedian. Kaye himself tells the rest of the story of *Two by Two,* which opened on Broadway in November 1970:

> I know perfectly well that the kids who made "Hair" a hit aren't going to rush to see me. I don't blame 'em. Why should they go to the theater, what's it saying to them? I miss the kids, though. And maybe, just maybe, they'll hear we're doing an unusual show that's saying there was *always* a generation gap. There were revolutionaries in Noah's time . . .
>
> Dick Rodgers said, "How about a musical of 'The Flowering Peach?' " I wasn't convinced, though, until Dick and Peter Stone, who wrote our book, explained their concept: doing a musical with only eight people, the same as in the play, and having Noah start out as an old man, and then become young, and end up old again . . . I was excited, the idea seemed so—dangerous.[4]

Two by Two, in the musical dramatization by Peter Stone, begins with Noah on his six hundredth birthday, receiving the news from God that he is abandoning the human experiment as a bad job and will destroy it in a great flood. Flood scenes projected on a backdrop screen allow the audience to participate in this communication. The Old Testament instructions as to the Ark and the animals are communicated telepathically.

Two by Two.   Courtesy Frank Goodman, press agent.

Thus quickly is established the bond between actors and audience. They are living under the threat of the imminent destruction of all living things. So are we. Noah, his wife Esther, his sons Shem, Ham, and Japheth, their mates Rachel, Goldie, and Leah, now struggle to work out their reactions to this unprecedented situation, each according to his own personality—just as we do. Japheth, the youngest, is outraged by so ruthless an act of God. He threatens to stay behind when the Ark sails, and drown in protest. Noah, the authoritarian, attempts to enforce the ancient customs in the face of novel and desperate situations. Esther sees human survival as family survival. She rates the love of man and woman above inscribed law, and will defend it even if it means so drastic a break with custom as divorce and remarriage. Ham, the adulterer, makes just such a break necessary by his inability to control his lust. Shem, the commercial opportunist, cannot conceive a world where the accumulation of money and possessions is not the paramount goal.

The resolution is most thoroughly Jungian. Noah, representing man, and God make a "covenant" in which both agree to change. God agrees not to annihilate mankind again; man agrees to be a more humane and responsible custodian of the Earth. The relation between man and God is revealed as an evolutionary one, in which both parties change and grow. Their growth is in the direction of a more loving, more just, more compassionate comprehension—which is exactly the thrust of Jung's book *Answer to Job.*

The themei of *Fiddler on the Roof,* the musical based on Sholem Aleichem's stories (dramatized by Joseph Stein) also involves a faithful man of God caught with his family in a scene of cataclysmic change. Tevye is a dairyman in the Russian village of Anatevka. He has a wife and five daughters. The time at the raising of the curtain is 1905, and the action sweeps the family through the pogroms, dislocations, broken loyalties, and shattered traditions caused by the prerevolutionary upheavals of the following years. Again the theme is change: change in man and change in God. Here the mode of communication is prayer—the simple, audible, spontaneous one-sided

Fiddler on the Roof. Photo by Friedman-Abeles. Courtesy Sol Jacobson, press agent.

dialogue (God's responses are silent and telepathic) between a man of faith and his God. *Fiddler on the Roof* opened on Broadway in 1964 and as this is written (1970) is still running in New York, in London, and on the road.

Hadrian VII is as rigidly Roman Catholic in milieu as the offerings just mentioned are thoroughly Jewish. The theme is again change. Again God is immanently present in the affairs of man. But in *Hadrian VII* the divine presence or absence is manifested only in professed human loyalties, institutions, actions, rituals, and events. Nobody talks to God except in formal prayer. If God answers, his answer is more likely to come through events—usually unexpected—than through direct and personal give-and-take.

The story concerns a destitute and neurotic English writer obsessed with a passion to become a Roman Catholic priest. The hopeless confrontations of his erratic nature with the stylized customs of the church have produced years of trials and frustrations, but no access to the priesthood. As he sits waiting to be evicted from his London furnished room a powerful fantasy overtakes him, which he feverishly begins to write down. The rest of the play is the fantasy.

In the fantasy, which has now taken on stage reality, high emmissaries of the church approach him in humble mission to redress past wrongs. He graciously accepts, is made a priest, and goes to Rome as private chaplain to one of the English cardinals in attendance at the conclave to elect a new pope. This convocation, it turns out, is hopelessly deadlocked in factional rivalry. No faction will yield, and none can muster enough votes to elect a pope. The only alternatives are to do without a pope or elect a dark horse uncommitted to any faction. The English cardinal nominates his recently ordained chaplain, who is elected pope. After the initial shock this worthy regains his poise, designates himself Hadrian VII, regally takes over the papacy, and proceeds to remake the church to accord with ideas he has long cherished. His sweeping reforms in the direction of humanizing and spiritualizing a church grown callous, institutional, and secular cause him difficulties, of course. But he overcomes them all, and crowns his papacy with the following speech:

Wherefore Most Eminent Lords and Venerable Fathers, let not the sheep of Christ's flock be neglected while the shepherds exchange anathemas. Try, Venerable Fathers, to believe that the time has come for taking stock. Ask yourselves whether we really are as successful as we think we are—whether in fact we are not abject and lamentable failures in the eyes of God. We have added and added to the riches, pomp and power of the Church, yet everywhere there is great wealth alongside dire poverty; there are stong nations brutally holding small ones to slavery; above all there are millions of people of goodwill looking to us for moral and spiritual leadership who get from us only dogmatic interpretations of canon law in return. If, then, we have so far failed in spreading Christ's Gospel, let us try anew. Let us try the road of Apostolic simplicity—the simplicity of Peter the Fisherman. At least let us try.—Act Two, Scene Two[5]

Shortly following this utterance, Hadrian VII is assassinated by the agent of a fanatical Protestant sect. This shatters the fantasy and turns the pope back into a poverty-ridden London neurotic waiting to be evicted from his shabby room—a matter which a pair of the Queen's bailiffs promptly take care of. The effect is powerful. It calls for no metaphysical discussion—philosophical, theological, or psychological. It is a blunt and practical critique of a human institution which claims cosmic compassion as its inspiration and its aim.

Hadrian VII is a dramatization by Peter Luke of a novel of the same title published in 1904 by the eccentric British genius Frederick Rolfe. For those who enjoy literary oddities of bohemian flavor, antique patina, and rare quality, the writings produced and inspired by the extraordinary Rolfe provide an adventure. Rolfe was born to middle-class Anglican parents in 1860, ran away from his London home when he was fifteen, lived a life of abject poverty, and died in Venice at the age of fifty-three, under a cloud of rascality and homosexuality. Fascinated by the church, he tried for holy orders, held several teaching jobs under church auspices, and rendered various services (One of them was painting ecclesiastical banners.) to religious institutions. But his odd personality and fierce temper ended every relationship in bitter recrimination, and at last he was living by jumping from one precarious odd job to another. Rolfe was a many-faceted genius with astonishing precognitive powers. He pioneered underwater and flash photography and developed the theory of color photography two generations in advance of the technology of his day. He foresaw the Russian Revolution of 1917 in amazing detail, even to the slaughter of the ruling monarchs and their children. He wrote a number of books of quality and strange power. His masterpiece, *Hadrian the Seventh,* has been admired by writers of stature from D. H. Lawrence to Graham Greene. In 1934 A. J. A. Symons wrote a biography of Rolfe, *The Quest for Corvo,* which is a literary oddment of the very first quality. His flash of truth, communicated to playgoers of the 1970's—all conditioned by the career of Pope John XXIII and the current turmoil in world Catholicism—has had a dazzling impact. The play first appeared in London in 1968. It came to Broadway the following year and enjoyed long runs there and on the road.

Some will say, and not without reason, that to include the sensationally successful, endlessly running *Hair* (by Gerome Ragni and James Rado; opened off-Broadway 1967; motion picture planned for 1972) as a representation of God on Broadway is to stretch a point. Though I concede that its inclusion calls for justification, I insist that *Hair* not only belongs, but that it is the proper capstone for all that came before it and a harbinger of twenty-first century theology. The whole progress of twentieth-century stage theology has been from the metaphysical, philosophical, and abstract to the immediate, the concrete, and the tangible. There is a trend *away* from separateness from Deity ("What is God's intent and how do I relate to it?") toward unity with Deity ("This immediate activity has cosmic meaning; I am cosmic intent in action; and this action has the name evolution of consciousness.").

Neither the Noah of *Two by Two* nor the neurotic of *Hadrian VII* have to endure anything like the tortured theological conflicts of the Dion Anthony of *The Great God Brown.* Noah and Hadrian were

Hair. Photo: Culver Pictures, Inc.

placed in situations where they had to act, and that action *was* God's intent. In the case of Noah, the action led not only to a specific achievement in the stream of events, but to an enormous expansion of Noah's capacity for awareness. At the beginning of the play, Noah saw himself as the sole agent of God on Earth. At the end he was able to see that his argumentative wife Esther, his contentious son Japheth, and even the lustful Ham and the greedy Shem, were as authentic channels of God's will as he was. "Hadrian" saw with shattering clarity that his only possible contribution to cosmic purpose was to enter the event stream by committing an immaterial fantasy to material paper—which paper was rudely taken from him by unsympathetic hands, leaving him no assurance that it would ever be seen again. It was seen again, of course, and by millions. This fact, when combined with Rolfe's demonstrated precognitive powers, amply rewards those of us who like to see a large remainder of mystery and mysticism in our religious exercises.

In this sense of a felt participation in a cosmos that in its essence is holy, *Hair* qualifies as religious drama. Though God is never directly addressed (Does one talk to one's own bloodstream?) he is felt as a presence in the very materials of the drama. Though the rituals of formal religion are sometimes satirized, the feel of the piece is devout: "Without God, we'd be no more than bacteria breeding on a pebble in space—I have been sent to earth on a mission" (Act Two).[6] In general, people who forgo commercial advancement and material comfort to wear their hair long and cast off the coercions of a tainted society, are represented as superior to shaved and short-clipped business-military types. But the cosmic evolutionary work does not stop with being poor and growing hair. Even people in long hair and rags, it is discovered, can be vicious and cruel, and this is acknowledged as something that needs to be worked on. All love is shown as holy, including sex unblessed by matrimony. The universe is shown as holy, including inanimate things—stars, planets, waters. The thrust of the piece is to enlist the divine-human imagination in the great joint task of creating "a planet where the air is pure the river waters crystal bright," and where wars, crime, and hate have been replaced by happiness and love (Act Two). *Hair* gives us this vision as a project now being worked on, rather than as an "impossible dream." It presents the matter as practical, worthy of consideration by intelligent beings, worth undergoing poverty and ridicule to realize—if, for now, only partially. The double-triangle love situation and the overhanging menace of the draft serve well in forcing these considerations into the foreground.

Hair has not yet had the full benefit of scholarly appraisal. It has many crudities. It floats on something that may ultimately be identified as hysteria. It is primitive. But it has brought God to Broadway as resident in bone and marrow, lip and hair, tongue and groin, circumstance and adventure. This, it seems to me, embodies the best of the theological and psychological speculation of our century. Having come this close, I question whether God will ever again return to those shadowy realms whence he has so strongly emerged to command attention on the dusty, splintered, rough-and-tumble boards of Broadway.

» 9 «
Conclusions

From the foregoing discussion, five conclusions may be drawn:
1. Insofar as the American commercial theater is concerned, the current literary cliché that God and religion are dead literary issues in the twentieth century stands refuted by the evidence.
2. The various concepts of the nature of God are under the close and frequent scrutiny of the ablest reflective minds in the American commercial theater.
3. The psychology of C. G. Jung has proved a useful aid in man's twentieth-century reexamination of the nature of Deity. It provides a bridge of thought and a platform for dialogue large enough to accommodate, for purposes of discourse, the whole spectrum of ontological precepts, from Freudian atheistic logical positivism to orthodox Christian Thomism.
4. The dominant literary concepts of good and evil, opposite sides of the same double-faced coin according to Jungian psychology, have reversed their positions between the nineteenth and twentieth centuries. In the nineteenth, the good and the optimistic were dominant, the evil and the pessimistic were subordinate; in the twentieth, the evil and the pessimistic are dominant, the good and the optimistic are subordinate.

5. The evolution of consciousness toward greater awareness and compassion is increasingly seen as a goal in which human and cosmic forces join.

Our first point is intrinsic to the evidence and calls for no extensive discussion. If America's most celebrated playwrights from the twenties into the seventies choose God and religion as themes for their most thoughtful works, one cannot reasonably claim the topics are dead intellectual issues.

The second point, that the nature of God is under close literary scrutiny, calls for a closer look. The historical American conception of God is that he is immanent and transcendant—concerned with heavenly matters beyond the reach of the human mind and with everyday human concerns—and is always, unvaryingly good. Evil is attributed to other forces, human or Satanic. The twentieth-century view leans toward the possibility that Christlike saintliness and Satanic destructiveness may both be aspects of the same divine entity, which is seen to be in neurotic conflict within itself and in need of reflective human cooperation to resolve an essentially internal struggle. Edward Albee goes so far in *Tiny Alice* as to suggest that God is, indeed, entirely evil, except for some possible incidental modicum of good that may result from the sporadic distribution of large amounts of money. Archibald MacLeish, in *J.B.* is not so extreme. Though he does bring God to account for capricious cruelty, he leaves him aware of what he has done and in a mood to repent and make amends. Eugene O'Neill, in *The Great God Brown,* finds that evil, in the form of a certain amount of Dionysian drinking and sensuous love, is an essential element of the highest levels of creativity. Arthur Miller's central argument in *After the Fall* is that man must consciously come to terms with the unconscious evil in himself and in the cosmos. The protagonist in this play, stretching his arms for the crucifixion posture, finds himself short of Christ's capacity to sustain evil, but nonetheless constrained to endure the evil in himself and everywhere. Other instances in dramatic literature could be found to support Jung's central contention that opposites, including good-and-evil, never come singly, but invariably in pairs. In any event, our examination of the above playwrights has demonstrated that the pseudoconscious cosmic force traditionally called the good God is being reassessed with an eye to a possibility that God-and-Satan is a single cosmic psychic entity.

Point three, asserting the usefulness of Jung's psychology in assessing literary treatments of God, has been demonstrated throughout this text and does not call for extensive reiteration. The great merit of Jung's structure is its inclusiveness. For example, Jung's psychology embraces the entire psychology of Freud, hence need not offend Freudian devotees beyond pointing out that their master's edifice houses only a portion of psychic reality. Similarly, Jung's hypotheses allow full scope for the activities of all the major philosophies and religions, pointing out only that speculations about God ranging outside the clinically demonstrable archetypes of the personal and collective unconscious must remain matters of speculation and of faith.

The fourth point, concerning the reversal of polarity in the literary presentation of good and evil between the nineteenth and twentieth centuries, may be supported by examination of the general literature of the two centuries. In order to underscore this statement it is useful to refer again to Joseph Hillis Miller's *The Disappearance of God,* already mentioned in the Preface to the work in hand (see p. 9 above). In the final pages of his book, Miller comments on the condition of nineteenth-century intellectual believers as follows:

> [Gerard Manley] Hopkins, who seems so different from other nineteenth-century writers who suffered the absence of God, in reality ends in a similar place. Like so many of his contemporaries, he believes in God, but is unable to reach him. . . . The saving power can come, for him at least, only beyond the gates of death, as DeQuincey can rise again only at the moment of death, as Arnold waits in the vacuum between two worlds, and as Cathy and Heathcliff, in *Wuthering Heights,* must die to be reunited. . . .

Browning alone seems to have glimpsed the fact that the sad alternatives of nihilism and escape beyond the world could be evaded if man would only reject twenty-five hundred years of belief in the dualism of heaven and earth. . . . But Browning, like DeQuincey, Arnold, Hopkins and Emily Brontë, was stretched on the rack of a fading transcendentalism, and could reach a precarious unity only by the most extravagant stratagems of the spirit.[1]

It seems to the present writer that Professor Miller has failed to take into account what has actually happened in twentieth-century dramatic literature in the United States. Certainly his account of the nineteenth-century situation is accurate. Emersonian transcendentalism was given a vicious topspin by the general religious-scientific-political-industrial-optimistic orgy of the century. Pushing God more and more into the transcendental made him less and less immanent until finally, using Professor Miller's word, he seemed to "disappear" from the Earth. Herman Melville tried to restore the divine polarity by pointing out, in *Moby Dick* and in other works, the presence of evil in the mystery of the cosmos. But in the mania of optimistic transcendentalism Melville was brushed aside, forcing writers who felt obliged to believe that divinity was exclusively good to resort to "extravagant stratagems." Also, Professor Miller's reference to "the sad alternatives of nihilism and escape" finds support in the European absurdists and atheistic existentialists of our own day.

In America, another alternative has been found. Melville, ignored in the nineteenth century, has been exalted to the highest position in American letters in the twentieth. His great discovery, that God can remain immanent as well as transcendant if only man will accept as his prime metaphysical task the acceptance and integration of the element of evil in the cosmos, opened a new metaphysical vein that has been mined by American playwrights of the first rank throughout the twentieth century.

In the nineteenth century goodness and optimism were dominant in literature, evil and pessimism were submerged. In the twentieth century, evil and pessimism are dominant in literature, goodness and optimism are submerged. In both centuries, as in all centuries, both elements are present. American writers agree with the European absurdists that man, if he is to survive, must consciously confront the evil in the cosmos, in his midst, and in himself. The more pessimistic of the Europeans seem to feel that even if man were to confront it, his evil would still overwhelm him. With the exception of Edward Albee's work, no such nihilism is found in the American products here discussed. O'Neill finds a kind of rebirth even in death. Wilder assures us that the universe has a long-haul meaning, even though this may not at all times be visible to man. MacLeish gives us a Job who yet will love God though God slay him. Miller unabashedly calls us to confession and repentance. Chayefsky gives us a God who will be patient with man's experiments until man may become ready to cooperate. The American playwrights here examined allow a hope, though never a certainty, that if man will consciously confront his evil he may not be destroyed by it, but may bring it to terms. Not eliminate, abolish, exterminate it in the nineteenth-century manner, just bring it to terms.

NOTES

PREFACE

1. C. G. Jung, *Memories, Dreams, Reflections* (New York: Random House, 1961), p. 336.
2. *Religious Drama 3*, ed. Marvin Halverson (New York: Meridian Books, 1959), p. iv.
3. *Best American Plays, Fifth Series 1958–1963*, ed. John Gassner (New York: Crown Publishers, 1963), p. 555.
4. John Mason Brown, *Dramatis Personae: A Retrospective Show* (New York: The Viking Press, 1963), p. 43.
5. M. E. Rutenberg, "Edward Albee, Social Critic" (Doctor's thesis, Yale University School of Drama, New Haven, 1965), p. 5.
6. Joseph Hillis Miller, *The Disappearance of God* (Cambridge: Harvard University Press, 1963), p. 1.

CHAPTER 1

1. *Nine Plays by Eugene O'Neill*, ed. Joseph Wood Krutch (New York: The Modern Library, 1954), p. xvii.
2. *Ibid.*
3. Barrett H. Clark, *Eugene O'Neill: The Man and His Plays* (New York: Dover Publications, 1947), p. 10.
4. *Ibid.*, p. 25.
5. *Ibid.*
6. Krutch, *op. cit.*, p. xii.
7. Clark, *op. cit.*, pp. 11–12.
8. *Ibid.*, p. 76.
9. *Ibid.*, p. 149.
10. *Ibid.*, pp. 147–148.
11. *Ibid.*, p. 150.
12. *Ibid.*, p. 121.
13. *Ibid.*, p. 120.
14. *Ibid.*, p. 140.
15. *Ibid.*, p. 106.
16. *Ibid.*, p. 105.
17. Eugene O'Neill, *The Great God Brown* (New York: Random House,

Inc., Copyright 1954 by Carlotta Monterey O'Neill). Used by permission.
18. S. K. Winther, *Eugene O'Neill* (New York: Russell & Russell, 1961), p. 60.
19. Helen Muchnic, "The Irrelevancy of Belief: The Iceman and The Lower Depths," *O'Neill and His Plays: Four Decades of Criticism,* ed. Oscar Cargill, *et al.* (New York: New York University Press, 1961), p. 439.
20. Jung, *op. cit.,* p. 340.
21. Cargill, *op. cit.,* p. 408 ff.

CHAPTER 2

1. Malcolm Cowley (Introduction), *A Thornton Wilder Trio* (New York: Criterion Books, 1956), p. 13.
2. *The Modern Theater,* ed. Robert W. Corrigan (New York: The Macmillan Company, 1964), p. 1185.
3. Cowley, *op. cit.,* p. 3.
4. Travis Bogard, "The Comedy of Thornton Wilder," *Modern Drama: Essays in Criticism,* ed. Travis Bogard and William I. Oliver (New York: Oxford University Press, 1965), p. 372.
5. Cowley, *op. cit.,* p. 18.
6. Bogard, *op. cit.,* p. 362.
7. Corrigan, *op. cit.,* p. 1074.
8. Jung, *op. cit.,* p. 326.

CHAPTER 3

1. Gassner, *op. cit.,* p. xviii.
2. *Ibid.*
3. *Ibid.,* p. xxiii.
4. "Archibald MacLeish," Rollene Waterman, *Saturday Review,* Vol. XXVIII (March 8, 1958), p. 18.
5. C. G. Jung, *Answer to Job* (Cleveland: World Publishing Company, 1960), p. 21.
6. Archibald MacLeish, *J.B.* (Boston: Houghton Mifflin Co., © 1958 by Archibald MacLeish). Used by permission.
7. *Ibid.*
8. Jung, *Answer to Job,* p. 64.

CHAPTER 4

1. "Williams: 20 Years After 'Glass Menagerie,' " Joanne Stang, The New York *Times* Theater Section (March 28, 1965), p. 3.
2. "Man Named Tennessee," *Newsweek,* Vol. XLIX (April 1, 1957), p. 81.
3. Otto Rank, *Art and Artist* (New York: Tudor Publishing Company, 1932), p. 64.

4. Signi Falk, *Tennessee Williams* (New Haven: College and University Press, 1961), p. 164.
5. *Ibid.*, p. 22.
6. *Ibid.*, p. 30.
7. *Ibid.*, p. 163.
8. *Ibid.*, p. 182.
9. "The Season on Broadway," Louis Kronenberger, *The Best Plays of 1958–1959* (New York: Dodd, Mead & Company, 1959), p. 14.
10. Stang, *op. cit.*, p. 3.
11. Falk, *op. cit.*, p. 154.
12. *Ibid.*, p. 167.
13. From "Sailing to Byzantium" by William Butler Yeats, *Collected Poems* (New York: The Macmillan Company, © 1956). Used by permission.
14. Stang, *op. cit.*, p. 3.

Chapter 5

1. Corrigan, *op. cit.*, p. 1250.
2. Dennis Welland, *Arthur Miller* (New York: Grove Press, 1961), p. 120.
3. John Mason Brown, *op. cit.*, p. 30.
4. Corrigan, *op. cit.*, p. 1249.
5. *Ibid.*
6. *Ibid.*, p. 1248.
7. Welland, *op. cit.*, p. 86. Material taken from *The Crucible* by Arthur Miller, Copyright 1952, 1953 by Arthur Miller. Reprinted by permission of The Viking Press, Inc.
8. "A Foreword by the Author," Arthur Miller, *Saturday Evening Post*, 237th Year, Issue no. 4 (February 1, 1964), p. 32.
9. Jung, *Memories, Dreams, Reflections*, p. 336.
10. Arthur Miller, "A Foreword by the Author," p. 32.
11. *Ibid.*
12. From *After the Fall* by Arthur Miller, Copyright © 1964 by Arthur Miller. Reprinted by permission of The Viking Press, Inc.
13. Welland, *op. cit.*, p. 87.
14. Arthur Miller, "A Foreword by the Author," p. 32.
15. Jung, *Memories, Dreams, Reflections*, p. 326 ff.

Chapter 6

1. Edward Albee, "Introduction by the Playwright," *The Best Plays of 1964–1965*, ed. Otis L. Guernsey, Jr. (New York: Dodd, Mead & Co., Inc., 1965), p. 252.
2. *Ibid.*
3. *Time*, vol. 85, no. 2 (January 8, 1965), p. 32.
4. "The Play that Dare Not Speak Its Name," Philip Roth, *New York*

Review of Books, vol. 4, no. 2 (February 25, 1965), p. 4.
5. Rutenberg, op. cit., p. 152.
6. Albee, op. cit., p. 252.
7. Jung, Memories, Dreams, Reflections, p. 364.
8. Sigmund Freud, *Beyond the Pleasure Principle* (New York: Bantam Books, 1959), p. 110.
9. Jung, Memories, Dreams, Reflections, pp. 186–187.
10. Ibid., pp. 192–193.

CHAPTER 7

1. Paddy Chayefsky, *Gideon* (New York: Random House, Copyright 1962 by Carnegie Productions, Inc.). Used by permission.
2. Ibid.
3. Ibid.
4. Ibid.
5. Gassner, op. cit., p. 555.
6. Chayefsky, op. cit.
7. Ibid.
8. Jung, *Modern Man in Search of a Soul* (New York: Harcourt, Brace, Inc., 1933), p. 219.
9. Ibid., p. 220.
10. Chayefsky, op. cit.

CHAPTER 8

1. Edward Murray, *Clifford Odets: The Thirties and After* (New York: Frederick Ungar Publishing Co., Inc., 1968).
2. Ibid., pp. 7–8.
3. Franz E. Winkler, *Man: The Bridge Between Two Worlds* (New York: Harper & Row, Publishers, 1960), pp. 122–123.
4. "Just a Guy Who Can't Say Noah," Tom Burke, New York *Times* Theater Section (November 8, 1970), pp. 1, 3.
5. Peter Luke, *Hadrian The Seventh* (New York: Alfred A. Knopf, Inc., © 1969). Used by permission.
6. Gerome Ragni and James Rado, *Hair* (New York: Simon and Schuster, Copyright 1966 by Gerome Ragni and James Rado). Used by permission.

CHAPTER 9

1. Joseph Miller, op. cit., p. 359.